The Bible Will Be My Textbook

Raven M. Brown

ISBN 978-1-0980-8045-7 (paperback)
ISBN 978-1-0980-8046-4 (digital)

Christian Faith Publishing, Inc.
832 Park Avenue
Meadville, PA 16335
www.christianfaithpublishing.com

Cover concept by: Raven M. Brown

(The Bible belonged to my grandmother, Mrs. Ida Dinkins, and was given upon her transitioning)

Printed in the United States of America

Cover concept:

The Bible and Jesus are the Word.
The blood and water on the cover represents:
    the blood and water John saw coming out of Jesus's side when
he was pierced for our transgressions,
    the living water, baptismal water, cleansing water,
    the shedding of blood for the remission of sins.

> And almost all things are by the law purged with
> blood; and without shedding of blood is no
> remission. (Heb. 9:22)

> And there are three that bear witness in earth, the
> Spirit, and the water, and the blood: and these
> three agree in one. (1 John 5:8)

Foreword

I must begin with saying it is truly an honor to share this event with you about this young lady who became a great woman of God.

She was once in a very dark place in her life but was able to overcome the most miserable time in her life, the temptations, and the negativity from others in and out of her circle.

She has found her God-given abilities to conquer the darkness that once had a strong hold over her life. Although there were times throughout her life where she walked alone, she was drawn to God, and now walks in the newness of life, in the light she has found, unfolding the most powerful information about God, his Word, and the "end-times" that no one could ever comprehend.

As I began reading this book, it was as if there was a force that didn't want me to continue, but as I read each chapter, each paragraph, it was filled with the most powerful information ever, even though I've read these scriptures many times before in the Bible.

Because of the effect it had on her life and the things she saw being revealed in the eyes of her spirit, she realized that God wanted her to share this with the world.

This book talks about the darkness of Satan and the satanic forces that destroy the lives of people and how one's mind can be under control, causing them to think there is no hope.

It talks about the bondage of the mind and how a person feels trapped and imprisoned within themselves, but through God, one can be set free.

It releases a hunger and desire to change, to move from where you are, even if you have experienced the life-changing rebirth in your life or you think there is no hope.

As you read, you hear God speaking from her words.

After I had finished reading her book, along with the biblical scriptures she referenced, I am encouraged as a result, and I am more willing than ever to do what God has commissioned.

I pray as you read that your heart too will be set on fire with the eagerness to please the Lord.

This young lady, who once walked in a dark place in her life, is being used by God to help others out of the dark place of their life and into the light of salvation.

This great woman of God is none other than Ms. Raven Brown.

Raven, I say to you, "Continue to be used in this unique way; for you are chosen."

Lillie B. Sowell, Evangelist

Introduction

Though I wrote this at the end, I felt I should include this statement at the beginning so it is understood, "I am writing from a 'WE ALL can do better' place and not from a judgmental one."

Having covered (I don't know how many) spiritual miles on this twenty-five-plus-years walk, I've had my spiritual highs and my spiritual lows on this journey.

In an exchange of texts, I told a friend that I've had spiritual lows, and she said she believes we all have. I further said, "There have been times when it was hard to pray and read God's Word, but it never lasted long because it can't with his spirit inside me." Eventually, I get up, dust myself off, and throw myself back into the Word where I find comfort and my strength is renewed. I realized each time I hit a low and can't find strength to pray and read, it's actually the prayer and reading that renews my strength. In other words, when we go on a fast from prayer and reading, we become weak. Then when we pray and read, we are fed and nourished, thereby, strengthened, so these are things we can't afford to fast on. It's the abstaining that gets us weak, which reminds me of a T-shirt I bought about twenty years ago that read "7 days without prayer makes one weak."

Each one of us has a calling, and I feel writing to encourage and inform is one of mine, so I share what's been placed on my heart.

Everyone has been given a measure of talent and a gift, and when you don't use it, it is taken and given to someone who will use it. Read Matthew 25:15–30, especially verses 26–28. We see the word *slothful*. We can't be lazy with what we've been given, for we were given talents and gifts to be fruitful, give an increase, and to enhance.

Farmers, fishermen, cooks, etc., have the ability to have food for their families but also to sell and make a living. If one knows how to sew, they can save by making their own clothes and their family's but also sell to others for a living. If you know how to do hair, you save money but can also make money doing for others.

So many people have no direction because they are considering what other's expectations are for them, how society views things, or comparing themselves to someone else and their accomplishments; but we all need to tap into our own gifts, talents, skills, and abilities so we can be fruitful and make a living with what we've been given.

If you don't know what talent or gift you have, pray and ask God to reveal it. Ask God to stir up the gift inside as he often did with his children. (The reason the gift needs to be stirred up is because it has sat idle for so long, unused, and needs stirring up to regain full strength.)

I didn't grow up writing, but I've always been a thinker. When I was in my early twenties, I began reading the Bible and songs, raps, and poems started to flow from me. I didn't have any knowledge of that gift inside me. As I got older, my thinking evolved into writings that were longer, such as this writing. I had no prior desire or knowledge I would be a published author, but that is a gift I was given, by simply putting the compilation of thoughts into writing.

When I was in my mid to late teens, after repeatedly hearing "we all were created for a purpose," I feared dying without fulfilling mine.

As I continued to write this, I began to feel as if this could be my last writing, my legacy, my contribution to the earth, and the fulfilling of my purpose.

None of us should be merely existing but rather seeking to fulfill our purpose in life and finding ways to contribute to help people become better and make the world a better place for the next generation.

We are more than conquerors, were created just below the angels, and given dominion on earth. To be given dominion over the earth is a great responsibility that should be handled responsibly. This is why it is time to walk in our purpose. It's time to wake up and stop hitting "snooze." The time is at hand, and we can't afford to continue to sleep on our gifts, talents, and purpose.

We live in a different type of society where it's commonplace for teens to have babies, young girls and boys to get abducted, school shootings, mass shootings, and a heightened level of bullying, racism, and police shootings/killings; so we must find ways to improve our environment and hold

> We live in a different type of society where it's commonplace for teens to have babies, young girls and boys to get abducted, school-shoots, mass shootings and with a heightened level of bullying, racism and police shootings/killings.

people, politicians, and those in authority accountable.

I realize not all may agree or accept what I write, and I never try to force-feed my beliefs on another. (Generally, when someone is upset about what I say concerning scripture, I say, "I didn't write it. I just read it.") I realize the devil can rise up and work in people as he did entering Judas. Judas betrayed Jesus with a kiss. Peter denied Jesus three times. Jonah tried to flee from the Lord. Jesus, looking at Peter, said, "Get thee behind me Satan," addressing the culprit behind Peter's speech. This is why we are told to pray for our enemies and forgive because the enemy is not the physical person you see but the spiritual entity you can't see.

> For we wrestle not against flesh and blood, but against principalities, against powers, against rulers of darkness of this world, against spiritual wickedness in high *places*. (Eph. 6:12)

> But Peter said, An-a-ni'as, why hath Satan filled thine heart to lie to the Holy Ghost, and to keep back *part* of the price of land? (Acts 5:3)

In addition, I've pointed out in the past how the devil seeks to work through those in your inner circle. He knows when you spot your enemy a mile away, you prepare yourself to defend, but when you see family and friends, you welcome with open arms, embrace, and let your guard down which is why he uses them.

Biblical references: Judas in Jesus's inner circle, Peter denying Christ from the inner circle.

Today's references: The *Jerry Springer Show* and other shows where you hear "I can't believe my own sister," "I can't believe my best friend would do this to me," "And he's supposed to be my boy."

I've backslid, repented, and sought God's mercy and forgiveness.

The reason some of us backslide is because we cut off branches of sin and not the root. When the root remains, and we only cut off branches of sin, it has the ability to grow back and manifest in our thoughts, speech, and actions. The Bible says an unfruitful tree must be hewn down from the root.

What I mean when I say "we cut off branches of sin but keep the root" is some are delivered from drug abuse but still hang around the people they had done drugs with. Some who have gotten married will keep old photos of an "ex" and then send a "friend request" and will find themselves on their Facebook page, clicking "like" on a photo they posted, and one thing leads to another. Some have stopped engaging in sexual habits but keep the root (porn magazines, videos, or websites in their browser). The devil is always seeking ways to pull you from the Word back into the world when the root remains.

Some of us have positive people in our lives who make a deposit and some who constantly make withdrawals. If you constantly are around people who make withdrawals versus deposits, you will find yourself spent, low in spirit, energy, money, and motivation. Some people sow seeds, and then there are toxic people who sow weeds (negativity, division, and doubt). If we are to grow, we have to learn to prune. If you want your hair to grow, you cut off split ends. If you want a plant/tree to grow, you prune. If you want to grow, you must cut off unfruitful habits, toxic people and places that are not conducive to your walk.

At times, I've felt spiritually idle and like I could be doing more to spread God's word and to bring him glory.

There have been times when I've felt amputated from the body of Christ and when I've been grafted back in. So this is the place I write from to help someone because I know somebody (if not you, then someone you know) can relate and benefit from it.

We hear people say they are bruised but not broken.

Donny sung, "We fall down, but we get up."

Paul said,

> We are troubled on every side, yet not distressed;
> we are perplexed, but not in despair; Persecuted,
> but not forsaken; cast down, but not destroyed.
> (2 Cor. 4:8–9)

In this life, if you are walking in Christ, you have become all too familiar with trials, tribulations, temptations, and struggles (financial, marital, parental, occupational, habitual, etc.) and know the walk can be trying. Whenever we try to do right or be positive, the twins, Doubt and Distraction, show up and tag-team to hinder our productivity. Be mindful of this and stay focused.

As a child of God, our light is supposed to be shining bright in the midst of all this darkness.

We're supposed to stand out, not blend in and be camouflaged like a chameleon. We are set apart. It is written that we are a peculiar people, so our light should be shining bright.

> But ye *are* a chosen generation, a royal priest-
> hood, an holy nation, a peculiar people; that ye
> should shew forth the praises of him who hath
> called you out of darkness into his marvelous
> light. (1 Pet. 2:9)

In John 5:35, Jesus describes John's light as "burning and a shin-ing light."

It is important to examine our walk to see if our light is shining bright, if it is dim, if it has been extinguished, if it's a sensor light that doesn't stay on (in and out of season) but comes on with movement (on Saturdays/Sundays for church, on Tuesday/Wednesday for Bible study, around like-minded people or in private). Do we say grace when at the table of nonbelievers? Or is it like a streetlight that comes on when it starts to get dark? For example, the situation gets dark enough for the light to come on when a doctor finds a lump, when a grandson is facing a lengthy jail sentence, or when the planes went through the towers, causing many to act religious and pray together saying, "God bless America." In this manner, it is like a streetlight because it comes on when our situations get dark enough and hard to deal with, and we know we need intervention. It can also be like a pilot light that had been blown out by hardship or depression and needs to be reignited with prayer, a word of encouragement, inter-cession, or fellowship.

> The same followed Paul and us, and cried, say-
> ing, These men are the servants of the most high
> God, which shew unto us the way of salvation.
> (Acts 16:17)

When people see us, is this what they are saying? Are we show-ing them the way of salvation?

We are the world's example, and believe it or not, the world is watching us, examining us, scrutinizing us, looking for examples that we are no different from them.

We have to be bold because the world is bold. I like Acts 4:8 where it says "Peter, being full of the spirit" because this tells me he's getting ready to let loose. The Spirit is on him, and he's getting ready to tell it like it is, and we can't be afraid to tell it like it is. We have to stop worrying about hurting feelings and more concerned about souls being saved.

The world is bold and will tell you to stand when you are standing for what you believe in by kneeling.

They give rights to certain folks that negate the rights of Christians and put one's rights over another's.

Some of this that follows may make some of you feel uncomfortable because it touches an area you may need to deal with, and you feel called out, but God called us out of the world and will call us out when we aren't doing what he has called us to do.

You may get to a point where you see an area you need to deal with. You may get to a point where you stop and feel some areas aren't relevant and don't apply to you, but keep reading. Trust me, you will find your section and then your row, and when you get to your seat of where you are in life, own it, deal with it, be healed, and be blessed. If you should find someone in your seat, it's because they are going through the same situation, dealing with the same sin/transgression, or struggling in that same area. Know that you are not alone.

He doesn't want us to get comfortable with sin. Consider the #metoo movement that called out some and put them on blast. When we don't deal with it, it comes to light, so we might as well deal with it.

Be careful not to judge because the light will be shined on your mess, but correct the beam that is in your eye so that you can discuss the splinter in another's.

The reason I am writing is to point out and remind people that there are two laws by which man is governed: the law of the LORD and the law of the land, and I sought to convey the differences between God's law and man's—the Word and the World and how they are contrary one to another.

there are two laws by which man is governed: the law of the LORD and the law of the land and I sought to convey the difference between…the Word and the World & how they are contrary one to another. It is vital to know the difference so that you realize: a choice exist that you must make.

It is vital to know the difference so that you realize a choice exists that you must make.

> For to be carnally minded is death; but to be spiritually minded *is* life and peace. Because the carnal mind *is* enmity against God: for it is not subject to the law of God, neither indeed can be. (Rom 8:6–7)

Over the years, many people have become less aware or mindful of that, so this merely serves as a friendly reminder.

> No servant can serve two masters: for either he will hate the one, and love the other; or else he will hold to the one, and despise the other. Ye cannot serve God and mammon. (Luke 16:13)

It's either the Creator or the creature.

He'd rather you be cold or hot and not lukewarm. We are to be friends with God and in enmity with the world, which is why in my poetry book I wrote, "man cannot serve two masters, or his end will surely be a disaster."

In addition, I'm writing to those who have a good job, make good money, are in good health, and couldn't be happier because these are the ones who seem to think God is for the destitute, people in prison, for people with problems, etc. They don't appear to have a need to pray, attend church, or have a relationship with God because they seem self-assured, self-sufficient, and self-reliant, but that's as if saying you no longer need your parents because they've raised you, and now that you are grown and can do things yourself, you no longer need a relationship. This group seems to think they get along just fine without prayer and God.

> Behold, the days come, saith the Lord GOD, that I will send a famine in the land, not a famine of bread, nor a thirst for water, but of hearing the words of the LORD: And they shall wander from sea to sea, and from the north even to the east, they shall run to and fro to seek the word of the LORD, and shall not find it. (Amos 8:11–12)

> And then will I profess unto them, I never knew you: depart from me, ye that work iniquity. (Matt. 7:23)

> Not everyone who saith unto me, Lord, Lord shall enter into the kingdom of heaven; but he that doeth the will of my Father which is in heaven. (Matt. 7:21)

> Seek ye the LORD while he may be found; call ye upon him while he is near. (Isa. 55:6)

It's also written that some will turn to fables.

I realize this is a lot to think about, and most dare to go there, but a darker day is on the horizon, and people should be prepared spiritually.

> Don't just think & plan for your future, that's not promised, but for your eternity that is.

Don't just think and plan for your future—that's not promised—but for your eternity, that is.

When I was in my early twenties, I used to think I was too far gone to go to heaven, so I felt I should just live life according to how I saw fit. I wasn't bad in the sight of man or according to man's laws or standards but sinful by God's law.

Maybe some of you feel this way, but know, while you're out there being as bad as you wanna be, it is written, "where sin abounded; grace did much more abound." This doesn't mean you continue sinning against God because you are covered by grace, but you should know you are not too far gone in sin that you can't be saved by grace.

God's grace surpasses the sins you have committed. His grace is sufficient, and his Word, the Holy Bible, tells of many people who were like you and me, who made bad decisions and mistakes, used bad judgment, and outright sinned against God but found grace, mercy, and forgiveness as well as salvation.

> My people are destroyed for lack of knowledge: because thou hast rejected knowledge, I will also reject thee, that thou shalt be no priest to me: seeing thou hast forgotten the law of thy God, I will also forget thy children. (Hosea 4:6)

So let us accept knowledge so that we perish not.

> He that hath ears to hear, let him hear. (Matt. 11:15)

This scripture used to confuse me. When I was unlearned, I was like "everyone has ears," so it seemed to apply to everyone, but as I grew spiritually, I realized "ears to hear" meant you had a genuine desire to hear/understand; therefore, "who hath ears to hear, let him hear"—Matthew 13:9, Matthew 11:15, and Mark 4:9—means let those who have a genuine desire to hear, let him understand.

CHAPTER 1

Some of us have spiritual gifts that have been conceived in us prior to conception and from the womb but have yet to travail and have past gestation of walking in our purpose, in part due to demands and distractions.

How many have aspirations that have been placed on the back burner and are past gestation of achievement? Of promotion? Of healing? Of deliverance? Whether going back to school by a certain time, starting a family, having a child, opening a business or more importantly, fulfilling what we were created AND called to do?

We have so many demands placed on us that pull from many directions, leaving us spent, and there are so many distractions, until we start twenty projects and haven't seen any to completion. I know I have. My hope is that I get back to each thing that I've started and complete them one by one.

We have some who won't say when God has said to speak (as I heard a pastor say recently, "Been there, done that. Got the T-shirt and the hat"). We have some who won't do what God has said to do. We have some Moseses who have asked, "Who am I to perform this?" and have come up with excuses for why they can't. We have some Jonahs who don't want to go where God has said to go. We have some Sarahs who doubt in their heart what God said He will do and bring to pass and who try to bring God's plan about in their own way. God promised Isaac, but Sarah doubted in her heart, leaned to her own understanding, and had a premature birth, in terms of having the "son" Ishmael through her handmaid prior to the promised son, Isaac.

While talking to a friend about something I was very passionate about, she asked, "Are you on a roll?"

I laughed and said, "No, I'm trying to induce labor." I'm trying to induce labor in me, as well as others, so when it's all said and done, we can say,

> I have fought a good fight, I have finished *my* course, I have kept the faith: Henceforth there is laid up for me a crown of righteousness, which the Lord, the righteous judge, shall give me at that day: and not to me only, but unto all them also that love his appearing. (2 Tim. 4:7–8)

I hope to induce labor that will bring forth that which has been conceived in us by God; induce labor so that we operate in the faith that moves mountains and slays giants; induce labor so we exercise our gifts, travail and triumph, and bring forth good works, holy and acceptable in his sight; induce labor that causes us to walk in our purpose that was conceived in us from the beginning.

Around seventeen years ago, my cousin, who was pregnant, used to say, "I can't wait for this baby to be born," "I can't wait for this baby to come out." She and I used to *walk* at the marina to naturally induce labor.

Are you ready to walk into your season? Maybe you aren't carrying a baby but a burden or other baggage you want to release. Maybe it's not a baby you're holding but a grudge you want to pass. If you want to induce labor to bear spiritual fruit, *walk*.

Walk in the Spirit.

> *This* I say then, Walk in the Spirit, and ye shall not fulfil the lust of the flesh. For the flesh lusteth against the Spirit, and the Spirit against the flesh: and these are contrary the one to the other: so that ye cannot do the things that ye would. (Gal 5:16–17)

Walk in Christ.

> As ye have therefore received Christ Jesus the Lord, so walk ye in him. (Col. 2:6)

Walk as Christ walked.

> He that saith he abideth in him ought himself also to walk, even as he walked. (1 John 2:6)

Walk in truth.

> I have no greater joy than to hear that my children walk in truth. (3 John 1:4)

Walk in love.

> And walk in love, as Christ also hath loved us, and hath given himself for us an offering and a sacrifice to God for a sweetsmelling savour. (Eph. 5:2)

Walk by faith.

> For we walk by faith, not by sight. (2 Cor. 5:7)

Walk in his laws.

> Neither have we obeyed the voice of the LORD our God, to walk in his laws, which he set before us by his servants the prophets. (Dan. 9:10)

CHAPTER 2

Some of us live vibrant/robust lives but a mundane spiritual one, so it's time to address the elephant in the room (the obvious problem), poke the monster (to cause an awakening, reaction, and action), stir up the gift inside us, move mountains (the habit you have trouble breaking and whatever or whoever is your stumbling block that hinders your growth), conquer fears, for God hasn't given us the spirit of fear.

Greater is he that is in you than that which is in the world.

I remember Mystic, a female rapper from Oakland, California, rap, "We in full battle, but we asleep on the fields." And I thought, *How can people be on the battlefield sleep?* It's a powerful lyric that accurately assesses the state some are in. We are to be aware of the devices of our enemy (2 Cor. 2:10–11). Remember in the book of Job, Satan said he was going to and fro in the earth, and we are told he is seeking whom he can devour. Remember he sought to sift Peter.

> [A]nd he shall speak *great* words against the most
> High, and shall wear out the saints of the most
> High. (Dan. 7:25)

So we are warned; he is going to wear...us...out.

I feel worn out and torn, but it only provokes me to write to awake, encourage, inspire, regenerate, inform the saints, and implore to read God's Word—the Holy Bible.

Remember when some didn't want us to learn to read and write? Now we can read, write, and type.

I want to encourage those who feel amputated from the body of Christ, whether by your own doing or ostracized by the church for your conduct or by the way members look at you with judgment when you enter or how they make you feel, and to the ones who feel severed from their family for past behavior or by their own success (Eph. 1:4–5).

I had a family member who had been homeless, and he called one day on an extremely hard-to-bear winter day. I said to some relatives, "He never calls or asked for help, so the fact that he called means he realizes he can't do things by himself. He doesn't want to be alone, and we need to go ahead and be there for him." I further stressed, "We've tried hard love, so now it's time to flip it and love hard." By him calling, that was the beginning of him being grafted back into the family body.

> We've tried hard love, so now it's time to flip it and love hard.

Some are burn victims who need to be grafted back into a relationship by forgiving, having been burned by someone who was close, considered a friend, and who was dear to them, or the person who burned needs to be grafted back (forgiven) into a relationship.

Years ago, I had raked pine needles, pet fecal matter, weeds, etc., into a pile in the backyard. I deemed all that I had raked "useless" and "good for nothing," something I didn't need and had planned to discard upon emptying the green recycle bin on trash day.

As time passed, vibrant, healthy green blades began to spring up.

As I stood there, I thought of people we discard or defriend, that we deem "useless" and "good-for-nothing" and how we say "I don't need them in my life" or "they'll never change"; but that vibrant, healthy green grass showed me when God rains on or reigns in a person's life, he can create new life in them, that will cause them to be useful, fruitful, and productive.

Sometimes, when we discard people, it can be considered *selfish* because we are thinking *we* don't need *them*. Have we considered that they may need us? When we stop making something about ourselves and consider someone else, we may respond differently.

The reason I say this is because years ago, I was frustrated because the train I was waiting for was late. As I stood there complaining internally, I began to think about the times I was running late on my way to work and how I had hoped the train was a minute or two, sometimes even seconds, late so I could catch it. It was okay when I wanted it to run late but not when I was ready to go home. That was selfish. I then said to myself, "Maybe someone else needed it to run a minute or two late." At that point, I smiled at this revelation, relaxed, and waited patiently. I realized when you change your outlook,

> When you change your outlook, you change the outcome.

you change the outcome. Instead of getting frustrated, elevating your blood pressure and being selfish, relax and consider someone else, and the outcome will be fine.

I hope this grafts those who feel amputated back into the body of Christ, fellowship, and family by establishing or reestablishing connectivity and for burn victims to mend relationships.

Chapter 3

Paul reminds us in Ephesians 5:16 to make the most of our time because the days are evil.

On August 27, 2018, at two different times, I heard two pastors who spoke of this passage as well as a couple more regarding how we spend our time.

This reminded me of something I shared with the church a few months ago, how the time is at hand and how the time of harvest is now but the laborers are few, imploring all to labor by spreading the gospel. Not all are called to preach, teach, etc., but all who have breath has a testimony to share.

I painted the picture using my lemon tree. I have picked lemons when ripe, but when I allow time to lapse, I have picked some that were bruised. When additional time lapsed, I've picked some that had fallen and were bruised but I was still able to salvage them. I have also seen some that had fallen, rotted, and were not able to be used.

I likened it to the condition that we find people in. Some are without peace and seek the peace that surpasses all understanding. Some are without guidance and seek the Way, the Truth, and the Life. Some are ready for harvesting, some are bruised, some have fallen, but the laborers must catch them before they rot (die a spiritual death) because when God makes the final judgment, none will be on parole or probation. None will be able to get out for good behavior or time-served. None will be able to appeal his judgment. None will be on house arrest or with an ankle monitor. None will sit on death row for years/decades. New evidence or an eyewitness is not going to exonerate you, for his judgment is true and righteous. Plus, 2 Timothy 4:4 tells us they will turn their ears from the truth and will turn to fables.

In addition, before I began to read the Word, I pray and ask God to guide me to where I need to read so it is relevant to the moment.

The reason for this is because if something is going on in the world at the time, I don't need to start at Genesis or go to Revelation or to Psalms as they may not have anything to do with the current situation. Something might be going on in my country or a little closer—in my state, in my county, in my city, in my neighborhood, under my roof, in my family, or at my job—so I ask God for guidance on where I need to read now, my *daily* bread.

This particular time, I was lead to Amos 8:11–12.

> Behold, the days come, saith the Lord GOD, that
> I will send a famine in the land, not a famine of
> bread, nor a thirst for water, but of hearing the
> words of the LORD: And they shall wander from
> sea to sea, and from the north even to the east,
> they shall run to and fro to seek the word of the
> LORD, and shall not find it.

So we have to catch them prior, while their ears and minds are still open to hear, receive, and heed the truth.

Time is a valuable and precious commodity that can't be regained once lost. Use it wisely.

CHAPTER 4

I know I have, at times, felt spiritually idle, like I should be doing more.

We hear about stories in the news that depict a dark and evil state of humanity, not just in this country but throughout the world. We all see prophecy overwhelmingly being fulfilled.

It makes me wonder, with each death, how many knew or didn't know Christ? What Christians did they come in contact with that did or didn't tell them about Christ?

That makes me feel a sense of urgency and makes me want to be more about my Father's business, and we have to be because Satan is going down his bucket list (yes, he has one too):

- ✓ Parents killing their kids and/or spouse
- ✓ Kids killing their parents and/or siblings
- ✓ Wars and rumors of war
- ✓ People lacking natural affection
- ✓ People being lovers of themselves (taking selfies all day)
- ✓ People defacing God's image
  Tattoos. Genesis 1:26 says, "And God said, Let us make man in *our image* after *our likeness*" (emphasis mine). Lev 19:28 says, "Ye shall not make any cuttings in your flesh for the dead, nor print any marks upon you: I *am* the LORD."
- ✓ Human trafficking of women, boys, and girls for labor and as sex slaves
- ✓ Increased suicides as young as eight years old
- ✓ Removal of commandments and prayer from schools and courthouses

✓ Spreading false doctrine (through false prophets, teachers, and literature). A former pastor used to say, "Some was sent and some just went."
✓ Police killing unarmed and disabled citizens
✓ The murdering of Christians
✓ Christians being falsely accused and imprisoned
✓ Those in authority are lacking compassion and mercy
✓ Sowing division (Republicans versus Democrats, men versus women (in positions and salary), straight versus LGBTQI, White versus Black/Brown/Yellow, rich versus poor (1 percent versus 99 percent), religious division—Muslims, Christians, Catholics)
You "make America great again" with diverse unity, not division.
✓ Foolish and senseless gang murders
✓ Priest raping and molesting and cover-ups
✓ Alternative lifestyles
✓ Nations against nations
✓ False peace among nations and allies
✓ School and church shootings
✓ All things Antichrist in movies, video games, music, music videos, ads, etc.
✓ Bullying
✓ Domestic violence
✓ Mass shootings
✓ Increased acts of racism

Murderers, rapists, and suicide victims have become younger.

Within the last few months of 2018, I've read stories of a ten-year-old Wisconsin girl who killed a six-month-old boy, was arrested, appeared in court, and her bond was set at fifty thousand dollars. An eleven-year-old Arizona boy killed his grandmother, then himself, after she repeatedly told him to clean his room. A fifteen-year-old Florida boy strangled his mother to death after arguing over his low grades. An eight-year-old boy was suspended in Taylorsville, Indiana, after showing a "hit list" on the school bus. An eleven-year-old Ohio boy stole his mother's SUV for the second time, leading police on a high-speed chase, speeding down the wrong way. Two preteens (ages eleven and twelve) were arrested before they carried out their plan to kill up to fifteen people. They said the more they killed, they'd get to hell faster. They had planned to kill the smaller ones first "since they would put up the least resistance."

A transfemale was asked when his journey started, and he said when he was three or four, he asked his parents, "When do I get to be a girl?"

In China, they started the first day of kindergarten with women who were pole dancing.

Another article that was met with opposition dealt with a father who made his ten-year-old daughter walk five miles to school over the course of three days as punishment for bullying, after she was suspended from riding the school bus for the second time for bullying another child. He drove alongside of her as she walked.

I'm not sure why it was met with opposition. He drove alongside of her to ensure her safety. It was her fault that she could not ride the school bus and had her privileges revoked, and it should teach her and others that bullying is a very serious matter with grave consequences. (See the RIP section at the end where I mention three eight- and nine-year-olds who committed suicide after being bullied).

...bullying is a very serious matter with grave consequences. (See R.I.P. section at the end where I mention three 8 and 9-year olds who committed suicide after being bullied).

Another article was about a mother who had been arrested for allowing her ten-year-old son to get a tattoo, which she permitted because she got tired of him asking.

Another article spoke of a mother who cooks daily for her teenagers who are eighteen, sixteen, and fourteen or takes them out for fast food because they refuse to eat leftovers or to cook for themselves, and they insist on having freshly cooked meals daily.

What has happened to the youth? What has gotten into them? How do they lack compassion, mercy, innocence, and a regard for life at such a young age?

How has killing, mutilating, and promiscuity become commonplace among the youth?

We see part of the problem is the lack of responsible parenting as well as the influence of music, games, social media, and movies and what they are being exposed to.

> What has happened to the youth? What has gotten into them? How do they lack compassion, mercy, innocence & a regard for life at such a young age? How has killing, mutilating, and promiscuity become commonplace amongst the youth?

Even the beverages have sinister names: *Monster* (tells you to "drink and *release the beast*"), *Venom, Spider,* Rockstar *Revolt* (flavors: *Killer* Grape, *Killer* Citrus, etc. Makes you wonder what's in it).

The games have sinister names, music, and actions: *Mortal Kombat,* Call of Duty, *Grand Theft* Auto, *Angry* Birds, etc. Games exist where you can kill, maim, and *even sexually assault.*

When I mentioned the names of the drinks above and the names of the games, a friend said he likes playing *Mortal Kombat Annihilation.* I said, "See! Annihilation." There's a common theme with the agenda.

I looked the game up, and there is a character named Lightning God Rayden. The description reads, "Fueled by next-gen technology, Mortal Kombat X combines unparalleled, cinematic presentation with all new gameplay *to deliver* the *most brutal Kombat experience ever*" (emphasis mine).

I remember being hooked on Tetris to the point where I would see blocks falling in my sleep, and I would be trying to flip them.

Upon hearing of the abovementioned games, I wondered, *If I'm seeing blocks falling in my sleep and trying to flip them, what are young kids, teenagers, etc., seeing in their sleep playing those?*

I remember a friend's four- or five-year-old daughter telling me about the *bad dream* she had where the red bird from *Angry* Birds was trying to harm her.

In the past, I've said, "When we learned how to drive, we used a simulator. When people learn how to fly, they use a simulator." This is basically what these games are, and they are teaching/training strategic methods to methodically take life. (The games/videos simulate to cause player(s) to assimilate.) It systematically indoctrinates and desensitizes as you see blood and killings, slowly removing peace from you and a regard for life.

In the videos, people are fleeing from the police, crashing, and are carrying out destructive scenarios.

If this seems far-fetched, look at the news.

I read a story where after playing countless hours of video games, a teenager stole a car from his house, ran some people over, and randomly shot innocent people.

The mind, heart and spirit are the three most powerful assets a human being possesses and can be very destructive and altered when genetically engineered, modified, and chemically-induced by what we consume through our mouth, eyes, ears, heart, mind, and spirit, via food, alcohol and sugary beverages, smoking, drugs, vaping, suggestive images in ads, music, and video games, movies, etc.

I read another story about a man in Australia, I think, who went on a rampage, killing innocent people.

He said, at first, he started playing the games by himself, over twenty hours a day, then he started playing against other players on the internet. He said he got so good he could anticipate where law enforcement would come from. He said if he could do it over again, he could kill more. The way he said it was as if he was disappointed in himself for not accomplishing more and wished he could have another chance.

We used to play Pac-Man, Ms. Pac-Man, Space Invaders, etc., but I don't recall playing games where blood would splat.

In recent years, more violence has been placed in video games with rock and rap music blaring in the background, and they've enlisted rappers to add music to pump you up to incite emotions of anger to make you take pleasure in taking life, maiming, and causing destruction.

For those of you who have not seen the first *Ride Along* movie with Ice Cube and Kevin Hart, Kevin's character was playing a video game with several friends (probably internet made), and when his fiancée entered and attempted to turn it off, he explained, "Babe, you don't understand. I feel like I've been in Afghanistan for the last eight hours."

With virtual reality, many people feel like they are somewhere else. They have virtual reality headsets where you feel like you have visited somewhere else.

Many of the games are training for combat.

Even the dance moves resemble combat or sex.

CHAPTER 5

On September 9, 2018, I was on my way to Oakland and stopped by 7-Eleven. On the way in, a young man, who I later learned was twenty-four with a four-year-old daughter, asked me if I could support his CD for "only three dollars." I asked if it had profanity, and he said, "No, not like that. I'm no street n——. I rap about..." So I said okay and gave him three dollars.

Since I had to get gas, I listened on the way and on the way back. Even though I had plans to go to Oakland and could have hopped on the freeway, I felt it was important to let him know my thoughts. I drove back and let down my window and handed the CD back.

I said, "I like number 4. Number 1 was okay. Number 2 probably would be popular in this climate, but I really can't use the rest."

He asked if I wanted my money back.

I said, "No, you keep that. You asked me for support, but I'm a Christian (plus I revealed my age), and I like music with substance. We have enough songs rapping about sex, drugs, alcohol, material possessions, etc.. We don't need more of that." Then I got out of the car to further elaborate. "A lot is going on under this current administration. Blacks and Browns are being killed by police. Young people are committing suicide. Write from that place. There's so much going on. Write, drawing from your experiences and what you see in society."

He said, "Thank you. I appreciate you coming back and telling me what you thought. I'm going to consider that."

By the time we finished, he said he was going to write something new and wanted my opinion, so I agreed to read and give my opinion.

I told him that the next time I see him, I'd share my poems and raps. He said he'd like that. Remember, I still needed to get to Oakland. I told myself that I may never see this young man again, so I decided to go get the poetry book, poems, and raps that were not in the book.

As he read each one, in shock, he asked, "You wrote this?"

I told him that when I first started writing and before my conversion, I used some profanity in frustration and irritation of things I saw wrong in society, but they all had meaningful messages.

He said he really liked my poem "When I Look Into Our Daughter's Eyes" since he has a four-year-old daughter.

Upon hearing that, I told him, "You set the bar for your daughter. You are the first example of what she should look for in a man pursuing her heart and what qualities he should possess. Write with your daughter in mind."

Hopefully, our conversation will lead him to write something insightful that produces awareness and change for the youth; they need it. I've heard what they listen to, and I hear the N, B, and MF words a lot. I can tell it causes them to feel selfish, disrespectful, angry, and destructive.

When you see young kids, teenagers, and young adults on the wrong path, I encourage you to take the time, as I did, to drop some knowledge, sow a seed, and encourage. Don't think it's not your responsibility because it is. We have a responsibility to reach and teach. Don't assume they were raised.

Our youth are attacked in ways we've never been—by the devil, their peers, societal norms, or expectations. A boy's manhood is being tried. Kids are dared and challenged in ways we weren't.

Some of us may have been picked on, but we were stronger, having been raised. If you were picked on because you were nerdy or a geek, you resorted to hanging around other geeks. If you were a bookworm, you hung around other bookworms, retreated to the library, or you kept your head in a book. You didn't kill yourself. We were validated at the house, so we didn't seek it from others and weren't crushed when someone tried to belittle us. We knew how to rise above their insults.

So for those of you who have young children, teenagers, young adults, or grandchildren, raise them to have tough skin and prepare them for this new world because it is relentless, hateful, unapologetic and unremorseful.

Children are being bullied by classmates and even by parents of classmates. I've read stories where a parent has sent messages on Facebook, telling a child they should just kill themselves, not to mention Fox News reporters who attacked the Parkland School teenage survivors. When did it become okay for adults to verbally attack and demean kids? But it's Sly Fox News, so what can we expect?

Now that many states have legalized marijuana and marijuana edibles, *do you tell your child its wrong?*

Being a parent has always been a challenge, but now it's more difficult as the needle on the moral compass has moved to the low end. Are parents, particularly young ones, prepared to address these changes? Not to mention it is becoming mandatory to vaccinate your child for school enrollment.

People have asked me throughout the years if I wanted to have a child. I have gone from "yes" to "no" to "maybe" to "not in this country" to "only if it's God's will." But if it's up to me, I'm good; no, thanks.

There's just so much going on here that parents have opted to homeschool or place their kids in a charter school where they, unconventionally, teach.

Back in the day, children could go to school and learn. Now they have to use clear backpacks to make sure they don't contain weapons. Back when I went to school, we had earthquake and fire drills so that we would know what to do in case one occurred. Now they have drills at the school in the event an "active shooter" is on school grounds, and there are discussions of whether teachers

Back when I went to school, we had earthquake & fire drills so that we would know what to do in case one occurred. Now, they have drills at the school in the event an "active shooter" is on school grounds & there are discussions of whether teachers should be allowed to have a gun in the classroom.

should be allowed to have a gun in the classroom and should some be allowed to have guns in the church.

Back then, people protested war and women's rights. Now you have children protesting gun laws because their classmates and faculty are being killed at the school.

So I hope to encourage those who have felt spiritually idle or feel like they've been living a spiritually mundane life.

In addition to meeting him, on September 8, 2018, I met a sixty-four-year-old who, after a couple of days of conversing, asked where she could buy a Bible. We had planned to go to a store that upcoming weekend.

God is still moving. Jesus said,

> The harvest truly is plenteous, but the labourers
> are few; Pray ye therefore the Lord of the harvest,
> that he will send forth labourers into his harvest.
> (Matt. 9:37–38)

Chapter 6

In talking to the same friend mentioned earlier who asked if I was on a roll, I explained how I've heard parents say that there isn't a manual for raising kids or a manual for marriage, and she jokingly asked if I was going to write one. I explained to her that one had already been written.

Whenever you buy an appliance, a vehicle, etc., it comes with a manual or may read "Operating Manual."

A manual usually cautions you to read the entire manual before using and covers instructions to operate in some of these areas:

- Safety and hazards that may result in injury or death
- How to maintain
- How to clean
- Troubleshooting
- How to get optimal performance/maximize results
- Dos and don'ts
- Guarantees and return policy
- Warranty (lifetime or limited)
- What voids the warranty

Nowadays, most manuals come in several languages.

If a manufacturer, designer, etc., of a product/appliance has sense enough to provide a manual to cover what they have made, don't you think the Creator would provide us a manual, so to speak, for all he created, knowing the adversities, dilemmas, trials and tribulations, temptations, struggles, loss, grief, complexities of life, etc., that we would face?

The Bible includes instructions for safety and caution for hazardous conditions that may result in injury, execution/death, dos and don'ts ("thou shall" and "thou shalt not" commandments), how to clean (fast and pray), how to get optimal performance out of life, relationships, your body and health, your children, your spouse, your career, and how to troubleshoot (fast and pray, repent, confess our sins, forgive). And it comes with a guarantee policy (promises) and a return policy:

> Therefore if any man *be* in Christ, *he* is a new creature: old things are passed away; behold, all things are become new. (2 Cor. 5:17)

It also includes warranty, some with lifetime warranty—salvation/eternal life.

> [b]ut the gift of God *is* eternal life through Jesus Christ our Lord. (Rom. 6:23)

Sometimes there's a limited warranty that expires when you do—eternal damnation—and it also includes what will void the warranty—those who deny him, he will deny before the Father. Those who gain their life will lose it, a life with the absence of God, blasphemy of the Holy Ghost, and sinful conduct/iniquity without repentance.

> For the wages of sin is death. (Rom. 6:23)

> Wherefore I say unto you, All manner of sin and blasphemy shall be forgiven unto men: but the blasphemy *against* the *Holy* Ghost shall not be forgiven unto men. (Matt. 12:31)

Man is provided a number to call for assistance. We have prayer. Man has been given a table of contents to go right to a certain area of interest, concern, and question. God's table of contents has:

1) books of the Bible (Old and New Testament),
2) a concordance; and

3) from Genesis to Revelation, we are given where to turn for help through prayer, fellowship, fasting and praying, the elders, pastors, and the Good Shepherd, etc.

Dos:

- Love the Lord with all your heart, all your soul, all your strength, and all your mind.
- Seek ye first the kingdom of God, and his righteousness; and all these things will be added unto you.
- Cast your cares upon me.
- Look to the hills to which cometh your help.
- That men ought always to pray, and not faint...
- Study to show thyself approved.
- Be not afraid.
- Repent and be baptized.
- Put on the whole armour of God.
- Seek and ye shall find, knock and the door will be opened unto you.
- Be ye merciful as your Father in heaven is merciful.
- Submit to God, resist the devil and he will flee.
- Pick up your cross and follow me.
- Seek ye wisdom, and in all thy getting, get understanding.
- Pray without ceasing.
- Eschew evil and do good.
- Make no provisions for the flesh.
- Bring ye all the tithes into the storehouse, that there may be meat in mine house...
- Let us therefore fear, lest, a promise being left us of entering into his rest, any of you should seem to come short of it.
- Count it all joy when ye shall fall into divers temptation; knowing this, that the trying of your faith worketh patience.
- Love thy neighbor.
- Be anxious over nothing.
- O taste and see that the Lord is good.
- Watch and pray that ye enter not into temptation.

- Pray for your enemy. (Jesus washed Judas's feet, along with the other disciples, though he knew he'd betray him. God told us to pray for our enemies because He knew we would perceive the person we had an issue with as an enemy, but there is only one enemy; that is the devil/Satan/the Serpent/Antichrist. Jesus looked at Peter and rebuked him, saying, "Satan get thee behind me," knowing the spirit that operated in him. We have to stop looking at the person and start rebuking the spirit behind them.)
- If any of you lack wisdom, let him ask of God, that giveth to all men liberally, and upbraideth not; and it shall be given him.
- Present your bodies a living sacrifice, holy, acceptable unto God, which is your reasonable service.
- Be ye transformed by the renewing of your mind…
- Be not forgetful to entertain strangers: for thereby some have entertained angels unawares.

Don'ts:

- Lean not to thy own understanding, but in all thy ways, acknowledge Him and he will direct thy path.
- Let no man deceive you by any means.
- Thou shall have no other gods before me.
- Let not your heart be troubled.
- Don't let the sun go down on your anger.
- Only *use* not liberty for an occasion to the flesh…
- Don't be deceived, God is not mocked.
- Be not wise in thine own eyes: fear the LORD, and depart from evil.
- Be not conformed to this world.

Troubleshooting:

Repent

On September 23, 2018, I heard a minister say repenting isn't merely apologizing to God, but it is being converted from that sin.

Fast and pray

On the week of September 17, 2018, after mentioning fasting to a coworker, she asked what religion fasts and prays and the purpose. We ran out of time, so I didn't have time to explain to her fully, but here's the full explanation based on my own experience of fasting and praying.

It is written that we have the fruit of the flesh and the fruit of the Spirit, which can be found in Galatians 5:19–22. They are contrary to another and war against each other all day.

What you feed will grow. What you starve will die. When I fast and pray, my body gets weak, but my spirit gets stronger. The longer I fast, the more my spirit is strengthened, and I become more focused on spiritual matters and become more disciplined, making it easier to withstand temptations. *Fasting* and *praying* helps prevent this from occurring:

> Let not sin therefore reign in your mortal body, that ye should obey it in the lusts thereof. (Rom. 6:12)

The same coworker and I were having a discussion about gluttony which she wasn't clear on, so I explained to her that gluttony pertains to an excessive appetite that applies not only to food but also applies to an excessive appetite for sex, shopping, social media, video games, drinking, doing drugs, gambling, work (workaholics) etc. Some people binge on porn, watching TV, etc.

The world has eating contests to see who can eat the most pies, hotdogs, etc., while people are starving around the world, not to mention all the diseases that are a direct result of gluttony. (I read where a woman had found maggots in the folds of her flesh). There are video game marathons where people play for 12–24 hours or so and Forbes lists for those who are addicted to making money and making the list.

Confess your sins one to another

Some of us wear a mask and put on a front but are carrying around baggage.

I told a cousin about thirteen or fourteen years ago to let go of the weight she was carrying. "As a loved one, I can help you carry the load, but why not sit it down and let your ship sail? Some people have an anchor of anger, an anchor of guilt, an anchor of bitterness, of shame, of doubt, etc., that keeps them at bay. Why not cut the anchor and let your ship sail? Anchors keep you down, hold you back, as well as keep you unproductive and idle."

When we keep it inside, it has the ability to fester and manifest in the forms of depression, high blood pressure, ulcers, cancer and can cause bitterness, anger, shame, guilt and lead to excessive eating, chain-smoking, binge drinking, and other destructive behavior.

Some aren't just hiding sins; some are hiding problems, addictions, pain, and depression, which we are now learning after a suicide or an overdose. It is not until we remove the mask, be honest with ourselves and others (could be someone we are close to and/or a professional), and be transparent by revealing what's underneath that we can start the healing process.

I've met people who have what I call an emotional quilt with patches of *dis*honor. It seems they carry it around like a security blanket of all the misfortunes, mistakes, regrets, and everything negative that has been done to them. Not only do they feel sorry for themselves, but they want you to.

Guarantees (promises):

Come all ye that labour and I will give you rest.
(Matt 11:28)

He who waits on the Lord will renew his strength.
(Is 40:31).

Open you the windows of heaven, and pour you out a blessing, that there shall not be room enough to receive it. (Mal 3:10)

If my people, which are called by my name, shall humble themselves, and pray, and seek my face, and turn from their wicked ways; then will I hear from heaven, and will forgive their sin, and will heal their land. (2 Chron 7:14)

[T]hou wilt keep him in perfect peace. (Is 26:3)

I will never leave nor forsake you. (Heb 13:5).

[B]ut my God shall supply all your need. (Phil 4:19)

I heard a pastor on the radio say, "He didn't say he would supply all your greed. He said 'all your needs.'"

And I give unto them eternal life; and they shall never perish, neither shall any *man* pluck them out of my hand. My Father, which gave them me, is greater than all; and no *man* is able to pluck *them* out of my Father's hand. (John 10:28–29)

In my Father's house are many mansions: if it *were* not so, I would have told you. I go to prepare a place for you. And if I go and prepare a place for you, I will come again, and receive you unto myself; that where I am, *there* ye may be also. (John 14:2–3)

For God so loved the world, that he gave his only begotten Son, that whosoever believeth in him should not perish, but have everlasting life. (John 3:16)

And Jesus said unto them, Verily I say unto you, that ye which have followed me, in the regeneration when the Son of man shall sit in the throne of his glory, ye also shall sit upon twelve thrones, judging the twelve tribes of Israel. And every one that hath forsaken houses, or brethren, or sisters, or father, or mother, or wife, or children, or lands for my name's sake, shall receive an hundredfold, and shall inherit everlasting life. (Matt19:28-29)

When thou passest through the waters, I *will be* with thee; and through the rivers, they shall not overflow thee: when thou walkest through the fire, thou shalt not be burned; neither shall the flame kindle upon thee. (Isa. 43:2)

This reminds me of Jonah when he was disobedient. There was still grace in his chastisement. God prepared a great fish. Jonah didn't have to swim in deep waters. He didn't drown. He didn't suffocate inside the great fish. He wasn't eaten. He didn't die of starvation or dehydration, and once let out, he was spit upon the land. Upon the land, in the blistering heat, God provided a gourd (a plant to provide Jonah shade) that didn't need a seed, watering, pruning, etc. Because he remained disobedient, God had a worm eat the gourd. We see God's grace, patience, love, mercy, lovingkindness, and longsuffering through it all.

While on the subject of Jonah, I'd like to point out as he tempted to flee in a ship with others who were going to Tarshish:

[B]ut the LORD sent out a great wind into the sea, and there was a mighty tempest in the sea, so that the ship was like to be broken. Then the mariners were afraid, and cried every man unto his god, and cast forth the wares… Then were the men exceedingly afraid, and said unto him, Why hast thou done this? For the men knew that he fled from the presence of the LORD, because he had told them. Wherefore they cried unto the LORD, and said, we beseech thee, O LORD, we beseech thee, let us not perish for this man's life, and lay not upon us innocent blood: for thou, O LORD, has done as it pleased thee. Then the men feared the Lord exceedingly, and offered a sacrifice unto the LORD, and made vows. (Jon. 1:4–16)

So in verse 5, they cried out to their "gods" (li'l g), but in verse 14, "they cried unto the LORD," "we beseech thee O LORD," and said, "For thou, O LORD." And they feared the Lord exceedingly, offered a sacrifice, and made a vow to the LORD.

Their faith in their li'l "g" was shaken, and they saw in their life-and-death situation that the li'l "g" was nowhere to be found, didn't exist, didn't care, or didn't have the power or ability to save, so they cried out to the True and Living God, the one that caused the tempest and has the power and ability to cause the wind to cease and the power to save.

And God saw their works, that they turned from their evil way; and God repented of the evil, that he had said that he would do unto them; and he did it not. (Jon. 3:10)

Nonbelievers can still come to their senses, turn from their evil ways, and be pardoned by God.

Blessed is the man that endureth temptation: for when he is tried, he shall receive the crown of life, which the Lord hath promised to them that love him. (James 1:12)

> Bring ye all the tithes into the storehouse, that
> there may be meat in mine house, and prove me
> now herewith, saith the LORD of hosts, if I will
> not open you the windows of heaven, and pour
> you out a blessing, that *there shall* not *be room,*
> enough *to receive it.* (Mal 3:10)

Note: how much you tithe is evidence of your measure of faith.

> Will a man rob God? Yet ye have robbed me. But
> ye say, Wherein have we robbed thee? In tithes
> and offerings. Ye *are* cursed with a curse: for ye
> have robbed me, *even* this whole nation. (Mal.
> 3:8–9)

Many years ago, I said to my father, "I can't afford to pay tithes."
He responded, "I can't afford not to."

That stuck with me and was a pivotal point of paying 10 percent. When you give 10 percent of your income, your actions say that you are stepping out in faith and trusting God to supply all your needs as he said he would. Note: it says *needs* and not *wants/desires.* Sometimes, the things we want are not the things we need.

Parents do the same thing. They may not buy you a name-brand shoe, but you will have shoes on your feet. They may not buy you a pizza and soda, but they will provide something to eat and drink.

When I first bought my house and after I had paid my bills, it seemed like I just barely had enough to live on, so when I got paid, I asked God to bless the remaining money and stretch it like he did the loaves of bread and fish. (This is where the "prove me now" comes in). I also needed some shoes. During those two weeks, I received a check in the mail for an overpayment (must have overcharged because I don't send extra money that exceeds the invoice amount), I found cash, a friend had me stop by to get some food that lasted throughout the two weeks without even knowing my situation, and I got two pairs of shoes (one free and the other for twenty dollars). By the time I got paid again, I still had money left from the last paycheck.

God is not man, nor is he slack concerning his word. You have to trust wholeheartedly and believe.

> [f]or every one that exalteth himself shall be abased; and he that humbleth himself shall be exalted. (Luke 18:14)

Warning:

> For the wrath of God is revealed from heaven against all ungodliness and unrighteousness of men, who hold the truth in unrighteousness. (Rom. 1:18–20)

> A double minded man is unstable in all his ways.

> Will a man rob God? Yet ye have robbed me. But ye say, Wherein have we robbed thee? In tithes and offerings. Ye *are* cursed with a curse: for ye have robbed me, *even* this whole nation. (Mal 3:8-9)

> Beware lest any man spoil you through philosophy and vain deceit, after the tradition of men, after the rudiments of the world, and not after Christ. (Col. 2:8)

Chapter 7

I'm not sure who coined the acronym, B-I-B-L-E., but it was my father who shared it with me.

Basic **I**nstruction **B**efore **L**eaving **E**arth

What parent does not instruct a child on behavior and rewards and disciplines when necessary? Parents have a go-by of rules they have set and standards the child needs to uphold. Employers have a standard of conduct, dress code and rules on sexual harassment, performance, loyalty, attendance, being trustworthy, reliable, defrauding, etc.

God's Word speaks about women wearing modest apparel (dress code) and for men not to be effeminate (dress code), keeping your word, dishonoring others and your body, lying, cheating, stealing, coveting, etc.

We follow the law of man but question the law of God. We follow laws at work, while driving, in public, etc., because we know if we break a law, it could result in an arrest, confinement, fines, citations, court appearance, legal and/or attorney fees, etc.

If rules of marriage are broken, people know it can result in separation, divorce, effect child(ren), sleep pattern, appetite, and lead to infidelity, etc.

If we break laws at work, we know it could result in suspension, reprimand, a write-up, loss of wages, termination, etc.

If we break laws in traffic, we know it can result in an accident, citation, death, traffic school, increase in insurance, etc.

If we break laws in school, we know it can result in not being able to participate in a sports activity, a loss of scholarship, a suspension, or being expelled, etc..

So why do we not regard breaking God's laws, ordinances, commandments, statutes, etc.? We break his without any regard of what it could result in.

All laws restrict or limit our behavior/conduct and are imposed for our benefit as well as others, but God's aren't only for a benefit but for our well-being and spiritual well-being in this life and the one to follow, which is why I said "I'm trying to induce labor" for it is written to "labour to enter into this rest."

> "I'm trying to induce labor", for it is written to "labour to enter into this rest."

In studying, I've discovered the Way, the Truth, and the Life, sound doctrine, wisdom, knowledge, understanding, guidance, and life. And what's written has given me all those things as well as discernment, peace, insight, comfort, and purpose.

Back to there not being a manual for raising a child or for marriage. I've read about celebrity parents and other parents who are practicing what they call *free-range parenting*, the concept of which is limited parental supervision that encourages children to function independently.

Recently, a mother had the police called on her after a concerned neighbor reported her for allowing her eight-year-old to walk the dog around the block without supervision.

The mother said she practices free-range parenting to teach independence, but in this day and age, we see children become the subjects of Amber Alerts, so maybe some should reconsider the way they apply this new concept, at what age, and under what circumstances.

Here are a few from "THEE manual" that not only deal with these relationships but other types as well:

> Train up a child in the way he should go: and when
> he is old, he will not depart from it. (Prov. 22:6)

He that spareth his rod hateth his son: but he that loveth him chasteneth him betimes. (Prov. 13:24)

Withhold not correction from the child: for *if* thou beatest him with the rod, he shall not die. Thou shalt beat him with the rod, and shalt deliver his soul from hell. (Prov. 23:13–14)

My son, keep thy father's commandment, and forsake not the law of thy mother. (Prov. 6:20)

Children, obey *your* parents in all things: for this is well pleasing unto the Lord. (Col. 3:20)

Read Romans 1:30.

Honour thy father and mother; which is the first commandment with promise; that it may be well with thee, and thou mayest live long on the earth. (Eph. 6:2–3)

But Jesus said, Suffer little children, and forbid them not, to come me: for of such is the kingdom of heaven. (Matt. 19:14)

Fathers, provoke not your children to *anger*, lest they be discouraged. (Col. 3:21)

And, ye fathers, provoke not your children to wrath: but bring them up in the nurture and admonition of the Lord. (Eph. 6:4)

Note: Think about how a parent loves their child(ren) but hates what they do. Our Father loves us but hates the sin we commit. You punish/discipline your child(ren) as does God his children.

A parent disciplines in such forms as no TV, cell phone, video games, participation in sports activity, restriction, etc., and some have kicked offspring out of the house. So if we do all this, how is it we don't expect God to discipline/chastise us? When parents discipline children, it's to punish for what they've done. When God disciplines, it's to teach discipline.

> When parents discipline children, it's to punish for what they've done. When God disciplines, it's to teach discipline.

I told a friend awhile back that when we were whooped, it put things in perspective. It quickly helped you assess what's important and worth it and what's not so important or worth it.

Not all children need a rod. Sometimes, the rod and staff provide guidance and protection as in "thy rod and staff, they comfort me."

Wives, submit yourselves unto your own husbands, as is fit in the Lord. (Col. 3:18)

Husbands, love *your* wives, and be not bitter against them. (Col. 3:19)

Husbands, love your wives, even as Christ also loved the church, and gave himself for it. (Eph. 5:25)

Nevertheless let every one of you in particular so love his wife even as himself; and the wife *see* that she reverence *her* husband. (Eph. 5:33)

So ought men to love their wives as their own bodies. He that loveth his wife loveth himself. (Eph. 5:28)

> Servants, obey in all things your masters according to the flesh; not with eyeservice, as menpleasers, but in singleness of heart, fearing God. (Col. 3:22)

> MASTERS, give unto *your* servants that which is just and equal; knowing that ye also have a Master in heaven. (Col. 4:1)

> Let the deacons be the husbands of one wife, ruling their children and household well. (1 Tim. 3:12)

> Even so *must their* wives *be* grave, not slanderers, sober, faithful in all things. (1 Tim 3:11)

In these examples, we see a two-way street. It's true for the children as well as the parent. ("Child" doesn't have an age limit and is extended until duration of life, so whether you are five or 50/10 or one hundred, it applies as long as your parent lives. I say this because people become "grown" and think that since they are adults, they can disrespect or that they are on the same level as the parent. Not ever.) This is also for the wife as well as the husband, for the servant as well as the master. There are many more scriptures that pertain to how to treat the poor, widows, the fatherless, those who reside safely with you, your neighbor, those you have problems with, those who have rule over you, etc. You will discover more as you study the manual for our lives.

> Now we exhort you, brethren, warn them that are unruly, comfort the feebleminded, support the weak, be patient toward all *men*. (1 Thess. 5:14)

> Forbearing one another, and forgiving one another, if any man have a quarrel against any: even as Christ forgave you, so also *do* ye. (Col. 3:13)

We have to not only learn to forgive others but forgive ourselves. We are not someone else's judge, nor are we our own, so we should stop judging ourselves so harshly.

I used to beat myself up and leave me for dead when I had failures and shortcomings, but I discovered that was not healthy. By living this way, you stunt your growth, and you spiral downward. Some go into depression.

Our mistakes, bad decisions, bad judgments, shortcomings, and imperfections are for us to learn lessons from, not to haunt us. We have to learn to throw these things, as well as unfruitful things, in what has been called "the sea of forgetfulness."

> Our mistakes, bad decisions, bad judgments, shortcomings & imperfections are for us to learn lessons from, not to haunt us.

I have observed the motion of the waves while at the beach, and they travel in one direction; they don't return. They stay flowing, so when you throw these things in the sea of forgetfulness, they don't return but rather get farther and farther away from you, so learn to let go and encourage yourself.

Many of us focus on what's holding us back versus what is going to pull us through. Some focus on things they don't have versus counting blessings for what they have, not considering the people who are less fortunate.

Two days before Thanksgiving of 2017, a camera was stolen off my house. I was hot/livid, and many ungodly thoughts quickly emerged and ran through my mind, but after relaxing and having time to think about it, God gave me a scripture letting me know he would take care of the person(s) responsible and that vengeance is his. Then he reminded me of Job, which quickly put everything into perspective. When I considered Job, I realized I hadn't suffered any real loss. I know many of you have read the book of Job, and some may not have, but when you are upset about loss of a job, wages, a family member, home, car, etc., consider Job, and you will quickly realize you haven't suffered any real loss. The majority of the time, we hear of "rags to riches" stories but seldom do we hear about "riches to rags." Job lost everything, to include: a clean bill of health, livestock, and ten children. This helped me count my blessings and not worry about the camera. It's material and can be replaced. I can't take it with me. That's why this is written:

> Lay not up for yourselves treasures upon earth, where moth and rust doth corrupt, *and where thieves break through and steal*: But lay up for yourselves treasures in heaven, where neither moth nor rust doth corrupt, *and where thieves do not break through nor steal*: For where your treasure is, there will be your heart also. (Matt. 6:19-21; italics mine)

CHAPTER 8

With all that goes on in the world and with opinions, practices, and laws changing, many people, to include Christians, have become confused, conflicted, and compromising. But we must remember, Satan said he wanted to be *like* the Most High, so we have to understand many things he does. Although some things he does are obviously Antichrist, some of his actions resemble God's, but don't be fooled.

> And no marvel; for Satan himself is transformed into an angel of light. (2 Cor. 11:14)

> Jesus Christ the same yesterday, and to day, and for ever. (Heb. 13:8)

I'm going to give some examples and show some of the differences between God's law and man's. On one side, you have the Word and the other side, the World. Even these two words are similar.

The Word says, "I am the Way, the Truth, and the Life and no one comes to the Father except by me."

Many religious groups and secret societies in disguise as religious groups claim to have *hidden truths* and *secret documents*, and in some cases, you have to belong to their society to obtain this *hidden secret*, whereas, God's Word is for all to read and study and to come to the knowledge of the truth.

The world says, "I'm living my Own truth" "I'm living my best life" "do you, boo" "I keep it 100" "my word is bond" "live *your* truth." And some say they are gods, not to mention all false doctrines and teachers to cause confusion and sow division. Make sure while you're living your "own" truth, it aligns with God's.

The world would also have you to believe you can hail someone else and tries to convince you to lift up man and tell you there is more than one way, *and there is*. It is written,

> There is a way which seemeth right unto a man, but the end thereof *are* the ways of death. (Prov. 14:12)

> [B]ehold, I set before you the way of life, and the way of death. (Jer. 21:8)

The Word says thou shall not commit fornication, thou shall not commit adultery as well as how to be with your OWN wife and your OWN husband.

The world, as long as you are two consenting adults, at the age of consent, agree to open marriage and engage in ménage à trois, be swingers, friends-with-benefits.

The Word says:

> And I say unto you, whosoever shall put away his wife, except *it be* for fornication, and shall marry another, committeth adultery: and whoso-ever marrieth her which is put away doth commit adultery. (Matt. 19:9)

The world says "I love you, but I'm not in love with you" "I just want to see other people" "This just no longer works for me" "It's not you. It's me." "I'm in love with someone else"—*irreconcilable differences*.

The Word says,

> Ye shall not make any cuttings in your flesh for the dead, nor print any marks upon you: I *am* the LORD. (Lev. 19:28)

The world encourages you to put graffiti on the temple (which your body is).

The Word says, "Vengeance is mine, saith the Lord." "Turn the other cheek" and "Recompense to no man evil for evil."

The world says, "Payback is a motha." And years ago, a female rapper/activist said, "Two wrongs don't make a right, but it sure makes us even."

The Word is against worshipping false idols and inanimate objects, those who practice witchcraft and sorcery, observers of times and zodiac signs/astrology, those who seek familiar spirits, divination, soothsayers.

> [T]hou shall not make unto thee any graven image, or any likeness of *any thing* that *is* in heaven above, or that *is* in earth beneath, or that *is* in the water under the earth: Thou shalt not bow down thyself to them, nor serve them: for I the LORD thy God *am* a jealous God: (Ex 20:4-5)

> What profiteth the graven image that the maker thereof hath graven it; the molten image, and a teacher of lies, that the maker of his work trusteth therein, to make dumb idols? Woe unto him that saith to the wood, Awake; to the dumb stone, Arise, it shall teach! Behold, it is laid over with gold and silver, and *there is* no breath at all in the midst of it. (Hab 2:18-19)

The world is into tarot cards and palm readers, psychics, Ouija boards, séance, fortune-telling, zodiac signs/astrology, clairvoyant, sun worshippers, worshippers of animals.

The Word calls it possession, spirits, demons.

The world calls it multiple personalities, split-personalities, schizophrenia, ghost.

The Word says, "Pray" "Fast and pray" "Pray for your enemy" "Prayer of the righteous availeth much."

The world says, "Make a wish" "Meditate," etc. A wish and meditation aren't the same as prayer. Some even bow down to inanimate objects, which also is spoken against in the Bible.

The Word says,

> And there came a voice to him, Rise, Peter; kill, and eat. (Acts 10:13)

> [W]hat God hath cleansed, *that* call not thou common. (15)

> And I heard a voice saying unto me, Arise, Peter; slay and eat. (11:7)

> But meat commendeth us not to God: for neither, if we eat, are we the better; neither, if we eat not, are we the worse. (1 Cor. 8:8)

> Not that which goeth into the mouth defileth a man; but that which cometh out of the mouth, this defileth a man. Do not ye yet understand, that whatsoever entereth in at the mouth goeth into the belly, and is cast out into the draught? But those things which proceed out of the mouth come forth from the heart; and they defile a man. For out of the heart proceed evil thoughts, murders, adulteries, fornications, thefts, false witness, blasphemies: These are the things which defile a man: but to eat with unwashen hands defileth not a man. (Matt. 15:11, 17–20)

The world doesn't eat meat or pork for religious reasons or because they feel it defiles their spirit.

The Word gives us examples of how God knows who we are before conception, during conception…and that the identity (name), the gender, and the purpose is known.

Examples:

In Luke 1:13, Zacharias was told his wife, Elisabeth, would bear a son (gender), to call his name John (identity). And verse 16 says, "And many of the children of Israel shall he turn to the Lord their God" (purpose). He was further told that John would "be filled with the Holy Ghost, even from his mother's womb," which is evident here: John, who was in his mother's (Elisabeth) womb, leaped inside when he heard the salutation of Mary, the mother of Jesus.

In Matthew 1:20–23, Joseph is told Mary is going to have a son (gender), they would call him "Jesus" (identity), and that he would save his people from sin (purpose). And it is said they will call him "Emmanuel" (identity), which is interpreted as "God with us," and he would be the Savior (purpose).

Rebekah wanted to know why she was experiencing discomfort in her body and asked God what it meant, and she was told she had two nations (twins) that were contrary to the other. The older would serve the younger. So Esau and Jacob were warring from the womb (war womb reminds me of the movie *War Room*).

In Jeremiah 1:5, the Lord told Jeremiah,

> Before I formed thee in the belly I knew thee;
> and before thou camest forth out of the womb
> I sanctified thee, *and* I ordained thee a prophet
> unto the nations.

The world tells you it's a woman's body, and it's for her to decide whether to keep or abort. The world also teaches that it's not a person but a fetus. I just read a story that read, "The fetus was 14 weeks."

This month, September 2018, I was listening to a Christian radio station, and they were saying how laws are changing regarding abortions and assisted dying because they harvest the organs and are using the organs from the babies for medical and scientific experiments. They allow abortions of babies up to thirty-two weeks so their parts can be SOLD for research.

That didn't surprise me as war is a major resource for harvesting.

In addition, I wonder why people are waiting to learn what the Supreme Court says about *abortion* when the Supreme Judge has already revealed to us in the previous examples that there's a person growing in the womb.

In the Bible, we have historical events of Pharaoh making it law that Hebrews be killed, which is why Moses's mom hid her *newborn*, Moses, in a basket. Herod also made it law to kill all children two and under in attempts to slaughter our King, Jesus, so today's abortion laws are not surprising or uncommon to the ungodly.

The Word says,

> Put on the whole armour of God, that ye may be able to stand against the wiles of the devil. For we wrestle not against flesh and blood, but against principalities, against powers, against the rulers of the darkness of this world, against spiritual wickedness in high *places*. Wherefore take unto you the whole armour of God, that ye may be able to withstand in the evil day, and having done all, to stand. (Eph. 6:11–13)

Continue to read Ephesians 6:11–18 to learn what the armor of God is.

The world tells you every one has the right to bear arms, but the enemy is spiritual and not physical.

The Word tells about God's commandments/statutes/ordinance.

The world looks to the constitution.

The Word reveals the Father, the Son, and the Holy Spirit, Jehovah, Wonderful, Counselor, Almighty, Omnipresent, Omnipotent, Messiah, I am, Yahweh, Adonai, El Shaddai, Elohim, Christ, Emmanuel, the Creator... and the world was created by God.

Time itself acknowledges his birth (BC—Before Christ).

> For unto us a child is born, unto us a son is given. (Isa. 9:6)

Jesus is the reason for the season.

The three wise men brought gifts of frankincense, myrrh, and gold to his impromptu baby shower. (There wasn't an exchange of gifts among everyone else, so why do children and adults make a list of things they want as if it's their birthday? How come people get upset or disappointed when they don't get what they want?)

How come people want to say "holiday" to include others so as not to offend them IF it's the celebration of Jesus's birth?

One of the biggest manufacturers of Christmas trees, which is located in Oregon, manufactures a million trees annually but refers to the trees as holiday trees, even though trees are not cut down or in artificial form for any of the holidays (New Year's, Martin Luther King Jr.'s Day, Presidents' Day, Easter, Memorial Day, Fourth of July, Labor Day, Veteran's Day, Thanksgiving, etc.)

Jesus is the Tree of Life, who was crucified, buried, and rose, so if he is the Tree of Life, why would you chop the tree down? What do the trees represent in this story?

They took prayer and the commandments out of the schools and the courthouses and Christ out of the holiday that's supposed to be celebrating his birth. That's like saying everyone is invited and welcomed to come to my birthday party, but I'm not invited or welcomed.

People rejoiced when Jesus was crucified, so why would we think his birthday is being celebrated by the masses?

When he was born, the king had all children two years old and under killed in an attempt to kill him. When it came to his fate, the people preferred to keep the thieves and said, in concert, "Crucify him, crucify him." So his birth wasn't celebrated by the masses, but his death was.

Then man came up with Christmas and later attached Christ's name but replaced it with Santa Claus and Easter and replaced Jesus with the rabbit to worship the fertility god.

The world seeks to make the *biggest profit of the year* off his birth while rejecting him at the same time by saying, "Happy Holiday" as to not offend others but rather offend him. They fear people more than God.

I don't know how someone could be offended by a God who left his throne, became flesh, dwelled among us, to bear our sins so that we would not be condemned. He was mocked, lied on, falsely accused, bruised for our transgressions and pierced for our iniquity, and by his stripes we are healed.

The world wants to say they believe in a higher power, the universe, evolution, the Big Bang Theory or are the follower of a man and wants to be omnipresent through technology by hearing and seeing everything so the powers that be feel "all-knowing." In addition, they want to bow down to inanimate objects made by man's hand.

> For as I passed by, and beheld your devotions, I found an altar with this inscription, To The Unknown God. Whom therefore ye ignorantly worship, him declare I unto you. (Acts 17:23)

Sadly, in today's society, you still have people worshiping an entity (unknown god) who they have no connection with, nor do they connect to the True and Living God.

A person can look at a car and marvel at the design. On the red carpet at an awards show, one can look at an elegant gown/dress or outfit and marvel at the design but not look at mankind/humans and marvel at the design. Nothing can evolve or "bang into" this type of perfection.

The body eliminates waste and toxins through the bowels, urine, saliva, mucus, and skin and has a vascular, respiratory, nervous, immune, muscular, etc., system. And nothing on the body is without a purpose, and this is true with every living being because they were created that way.

This design doesn't just happen. Each life has a counter mate of male and female to procreate.

For protection, some have poison, venom, claws, sharp teeth, shells, horns, beaks, or a spray, like a skunk. Some move by walking, sliding, swimming, flying, etc.

Not only were human beings created but all diverse birds, flowers, herbs, fruits, veggies, trees, plants, nuts, beans, grains, etc., then diverse lights such as stars, moon, sun, and the planets, etc.

Look at horses, zebras, donkeys, giraffes, antelopes, deer, moose, koala bears, black bears, brown bears, polar bears, pandas, etc., and lions, cougars, panthers, leopards, tigers, etc. and the birds. Each male and female pair still produces what they have always produced. (It's too much to go into in this writing, but before this writing took off in August 2018, I had started one on *Evolution vs. Creation*. I hope to resume after this one).

The Word says,

> Lay not up for yourselves treasures upon earth, where moth and rust doth corrupt, and where thieves break through and steal: But lay up for yourselves treasures in heaven, where neither moth nor rust doth corrupt, and where thieves do not break through nor steal: For where your treasure is, there will be your heart also. (Matt. 6:19–21)

> [F]or the love of money is the root of all evil: which while some coveted after, they have erred from the faith. (1 Tim. 6:10)

> For what shall it profit a man, if he shall gain the whole world, and lose his own soul? Or what shall a man give in exchange for his soul? (Mark 8:36–37)

I recently read a story about a well-known actress who is playing a Satanist. She refused to pray to him, saying, "It was bad enough I had to say 'hail Satan' a couple of times." She further stressed, "I'm a two-time cancer survivor, and I'm not gonna screw around with that."

> He must increase, but I *must* decrease. (John 3:30)

John realized that he must decrease in status, ministry, etc., and Jesus must increase.

Today, you have people operating as "the Jesus in me must decrease so that I can increase in fortune, fame, and possessions." You have people who are sacrificing and compromising their Christian faith and values for a contract in the entertainment industry. (Make sure "your soul" isn't in the fine print.)

Jesus was under forty but didn't seek to make a reputation for himself. He wasn't trying to be on "Forbes Richest 40 and Under," wasn't trying to go viral, did not have people serve him, nor did he exert his authority and power but humbled himself and served others, giving us an example. He didn't seek to rule with a power or ego trip but made righteous judgments and showed mercy and compassion, particularly to the poor, widowed, and those without a shepherd.

The world has rap songs like, "C.R.E.A.M." (**C**ash **R**ules **E**verything **A**round **M**e) and "Get Rich or Die Tryin'." There are shows that show houses and cars of the "Rich and Famous."

Judas betrayed Jesus for money.

The husband, An-a-ni'as, and his wife, Sapphira, sold a possession and kept back part of the price and yielded up the ghost for holding back money and then lying about it (Acts 5:1–10).

The prince of this world wants you to replace spiritual things with material things.

This is something to be mindful of because he seeks to steal your joy, peace, and soul and to hinder you from personal growth and fulfilling your dreams, goals, aspirations, achievements, and your purpose.

In addition, I'll point out again how the devil/Satan said he wanted to be like the Most High. An example is God wants us to submit ourselves as "a living sacrifice." Once God's unblemished Son offered and paid the ultimate sacrifice for the sins of mankind, animal sacrifice for sin was abolished.

> Then said Jesus unto his disciples, If any *man* will
> come after me, let him deny himself, and take up
> his cross, and follow me. (Matt. 16:24)

This sacrifice means you sacrifice what you would do or say to respond as God would have you. For instance, you may know something juicy or a secret, and you sacrifice versus gossiping. Or someone does something against you, and instead of seeking revenge to pay them back, you sacrifice and do what God would have you to do. Or an intimate situation arises, and instead of doing what you feel, you sacrifice and do what God would have you to do.

Now the devil/Satan, who wants to be "like the Most High," wants you to sacrifice too, except he demands/commands people to offer a dead sacrifice, where life has to be taken from a person and/or animal, and he wants your soul. (People, your soul is the life of you; don't sell it! Devil spelled backward is "lived"—past tense, dead spiritually, and he wants your company.)

> People, your soul is the life of you; don't sell it! Devil spelled backwards is "lived"—past tense, dead spiritually & he wants your company.

In Matthew 4:1–11, we are told as Jesus was ending his fast of forty days and nights, the devil showed him all the kingdoms and the glory thereof and offered it all to Jesus under the condition he'd fall down and worship him. (The devil is still making the same offer of careers, positions, status, riches, and fame in contracts in exchange for your soul.) Again it is said,

> For what shall it profit a man, if he shall gain the whole world, and lose his own soul? Or what shall a man give in exchange for his soul? (Mark 8:36–37)

The Word—make no molten or graven images of Jesus or idols to worship (Deut. 5:8, 6:4–5; Isa. 44:15; Exod. 20:4).

The world makes crucifixes and images they call depictions of Jesus, as well as other statues, stone, metal, and wood depictions of idols people worship.

The Word, in Genesis 9:11–17, is where God refers to a rainbow that he will set in the sky as a token of the covenant between

Him and the earth that he would not destroy all flesh again by flood. Stop! Read Ezekiel 1:28

In the world, the LGBTQ has made the rainbow a symbol of their pride.

God created man and woman, male and female of everything, and told them to be fruitful and multiply. God placed male and female of all living beings in the ark to be fruitful and multiply and replenish the earth after the flood. The Word helps us to be fruitful and multiply in childbearing, employment, health, and knowledge so we can positively impact others who are influenced by us.

Biology taught of two (2) chromosomes that determines gender—X=female and Y=male.

Satan said he can make male and female too and came up with transgender male, transgender female, nonconforming, nonbinary/gender binary, pansexual, asexual/agender, bi-gender, androgynous, intersex, etc. In some cases, you see "he was assigned at birth as" versus saying "he was born."

In the 2018 movie *The Mule*, which came out in December, Clint Eastwood's character interacted with a group of women on motorcycles, and one of them said, "We are Dykes on Bikes."

In LGBTQ, the Q stands for Queer, in which some identify.

So it appears that it is okay for some folks to refer to themselves as something but not for someone else to like the usage of the "N" word.

Blacks feel they can use it in an endearing way but take offense when others use it, so we are constantly seeing inconsistencies and double standards with words and actions as it pertains to the usage of the "N" word and "Queer" and other names LGBTQ identify with.

Rules need to be consistent and clean-cut.

The Word also has laws pertaining to marriage being between a man and a woman and against man with man, woman with woman, mankind and animal relations, incest, coveting another's wife/husband.

In the world, there's the song by Naughty by Nature saying, "you down with OPP" which stands for "other people's p——," "other people's p———," "other people's property," etc. (coveting and adultery).

California just passed a law that gives residents three (3) options for gender, and in some places, they want to pass a law where it gives the same fifty-three (53) options Facebook provides.

Makes you wonder if later there will be options to select human, humanoid, robot, vampire, cyborg, werewolf, etc. It's gotten that ridiculous. Last year, Saudi Arabia gave citizenship to a robot named Sophia. Mark Zuckerberg of Facebook had to destroy two AI robots because they (the robots) changed the font and language and started communicating with each other.

Back to where I was. The Bible says:

> Wherefore God also gave them up to uncleanness through the lusts of their own hearts, to dishonor their own bodies between themselves: Who changed the truth of God into a lie, and worshipped and served the creature more than the Creator, who is blessed for ever. Amen. For this cause God gave them up unto vile affections: for even their women did change the natural use into that which is against nature: And likewise also the men, leaving the natural use of the woman, burned in their lust one toward another; men with men working that which is unseemly, and receiving in themselves that recompence of their error which was meet. (Rom. 1:24-27)

> Know ye not that the unrighteous shall not inherit the kingdom of God? Be not deceived: neither fornicators, nor idolaters, nor adulterers, *nor effeminate, nor abusers of themselves with mankind,* nor thieves, nor covetous, nor drunkards, nor revilers, nor extortioners, shall inherit the kingdom of God. (1 Cor. 6:9–10; emphasis mine)

Thou shalt not lie with mankind, as with wom-
ankind: it *is* abomination. (Lev. 18:22)

If a man also lie with mankind, as he lieth with a
woman, both of them have committed an abomination: they shall surely be put to death; their
blood *shall be* upon them. (Lev. 20:13)

We all have sinned and come short of the glory of
God. (Rom. 3:23)

We are only saved by grace, and one sin doesn't trump another. Sins are equal in the sight of God.

The week of September 10, 2018, a teenage boy went to school with makeup and earrings, and he was sent home because it violated the school's dress code.

Of course, this was challenged, and the policy was called out-dated and double standard. Now a discussion of changing the policy is being considered. More than likely, they will not ban boys and girls from wearing makeup. In light of recent laws, it is likely they will allow boys to come to school the same way girls do, in continuation of breaking gender norms.

On September 24, 2018, I read a story where eighteen-year-old homeless high school football player, Jamal Speaks, was kicked off the football team in Washington, DC, after a principal learned he was homeless. Now this is a school policy that really deserves atten-tion and change. No one should be penalized for being homeless, especially a student who is there for an education and the opportu-nity to excel in areas he's passionate about that may lead to a lucrative deal that pulls him out of poverty.

In San Francisco, New York, and Los Angeles, they have Drag Queen Story Hour, where drag queens visit bookstores, libraries, and schools and teach the kids how to speak, dress, and apply makeup like a drag queen. In addition, they have coloring books with pictures of drag queens. They have a makeup booth and costumes and help the kids create a drag name to go by.

It's one thing if they are visiting these kids to teach tolerance and inclusion as well as to break down misconceptions and prejudice and to prevent hate crimes, such as bullying, beatings, and killings. I would understand that, but they are pushing a hard line, making a premeditated, calculated, deliberate attack on the youth. This is an agenda. Adults can make their own decisions. It goes past same-sex marriage, gender-neutral bathrooms, etc.

A drag queen who was doing the storytelling said, "I'm going to teach you how to say hello like a drag queen. Heeeeeeeeeeeeeeeeeeeee eeeeyyyyyyyy. Repeat after me."

He also said "hiiiiiiiiiiiiiiiiiiiiiiiiiieeeeeyy," and like I said above, they had costumes to dress up like them for the boys and girls. They applied makeup to the boys and girls and helped them create a drag name. This is indoctrination. They are targeting the youth. One baby was so young it couldn't walk and was standing up holding onto the table, while his parent sat behind him to prevent him from falling.

On December 5, 2018, I read a story about a mother in Kansas who pulled her two-year-old son from a private Christian preschool after she claims the school allowed the boy to wear a dress.

The mother said her girlfriend had dropped her son off at school and, shortly after, turned around to see him "parading around in a dress." The girlfriend then went back into the classroom, removed the dress, and said "We don't do this" in front of the teacher.

The mother said, "I am a lesbian, but I don't push my son in any direction. Whatever he decides to do or wear in the future is his decision."

According to the article, when the mother returned to speak to the teacher, she saw her son putting on the dress again while a teacher stood over him. The mother said, "I pulled his teacher aside and explained that I don't condone my son wearing a dress at school."

According to the mom, the teacher laughed and said, "He's only two!"

Apparently, it was for dress up, but it was learned they only supplied clothes for girls. The mother said her requests were disregarded, and because he was the only African American boy in the class, she feared possible discrimination.

According to the article, a representative for the school stated, "We encourage our children to play in a Christ-centered atmosphere that we hope will allow them to gain confidence."

> Know ye not that the unrighteous shall not inherit the kingdom of God? Be not deceived: neither fornicators, nor idolaters, nor adulterers, *nor effeminate, nor abusers of themselves with mankind.* (1 Cor 6:9; emphasis mine)

All religious-based schools/institutions have the responsibility to uphold God's word. It's one thing if the mother dressed her son in a dress and brought him to school, as long as it didn't violate a dress code, but it's another when a Christian school is encouraging it, supplying the dress, and going against the parent's wishes.

> All religious-based schools/institutions have the responsibility to uphold God's word.

According to the story, the mother, her girlfriend, and the boy's grandfather spoke to the school to no avail.

In addition, there were three other schools in the news that dealt with a lack of tolerance/acceptance.

A teacher at a Catholic high school in Pennsylvania was fired from her job as an English teacher where she had been employed for four years after she became pregnant by her boyfriend.

The Pope teaches that people should be more tolerant, and we have read many stories throughout the years of tolerance for priests who have not only done things contrary to the faith, sinned against God but have committed crimes, yet there was no tolerance or mercy for the unwed pregnant teacher.

Another story dealt with a teacher in New Jersey who was fired for not continuing to perpetuate a lie by telling first graders that Santa Claus wasn't real. It was also said that he told them that the Easter Bunny and Tooth Fairy were fake.

According to the article, the superintendent said "childhood wonder associated with all holidays and traditions" is special to her.

When I was a child, I read and heard stories about unicorns, mermaids, a pot of gold at the end of the tunnel, a four-leaf clover, and a rabbit's foot being lucky as well as hearing stories of Santa Claus, the Tooth Fairy, and the Easter Bunny, all things I grew out of.

As an adult, these are things I would be honest with my child(ren) about. I don't feel it ruins their childhood by knowing the truth. Truth empowers.

On December 9, 2018, I read a story about a Virginia High School teacher who was fired for refusing to use a transgender student's preferred pronouns, citing his Christian faith as the reason for his refusal.

According to the article, in a five-hour school board hearing, he said, "We are here today because a specific worldview is being imposed on me. Even higher than my family ranks my faith." When asked whether the debate was worth losing his job over, he responded, "There are some hills that are worth dying on."

On Friday, December 8, 2018, students at the school coordinated a walkout in support of the teacher and held signs that read "You can't impose delusion on us! #JusticeForVlaming" and "Men are men and women are women and that's a fact!"

We have three examples where Christians were (1) thrown in jail, (2) fired, and (3) sued in a case that went before the Supreme Court. So this tells us that in the Divided, oops, United States of America, the so-called Land of the Free, Christians are not free to exercise their religious freedoms.

God gave us a free will to do what we will, but man seeks to remove that free will.

I've read many stories where people have said there should be tolerance, yet for these teachers, tolerance and acceptance has not been extended. It seems there is a zero tolerance for those with Christian values or for beliefs that differ from certain agenda.

I don't feel either of the teachers should have been fired. In the first case, the Catholic school sends a message that there is no mercy, forgiveness, or room for errors, mistakes, accidents or bad judgment, and that everyone employed at that school is perfect and blameless before God.

In the second case, I feel the teacher should have been cautioned. Though he was telling the truth, it wasn't his place to tell the children, and they could have expressed that they would have liked for him to leave that to the parent to explain or for the child to find out on their own. If he continued to do that after the warning, maybe that would warrant further consideration.

We are constantly coming face-to-face with doubled standards and applying tolerance, acceptance, and inclusion where we want to as if there is no common ground or compromise. We should be consistent and not biased.

In the third case, why doesn't the teacher's religious views matter? What happened to his rights, or are they saying his do not matter? Are Christians a part of the "inclusion" concept?

Most employers have guidelines that state you cannot perform adverse actions against an employee based on gender, sexual orientation, age, religion, political views, national origin, etc., yet we keep seeing where people who exercise their faith are fired.

Are Christians going to continue to be fired and imprisoned for their beliefs/faith? I haven't heard anyone calling the Bible homophobic.

Also in recent days, stories about Kevin Hart (comedian) and Kyler Murray (Heisman Trophy winner) have clogged the news feeds. In both cases, tweets containing what some call "homophobic" language resurfaced. In Kevin Hart's case, they were made in 2009 and 2011. In Kyler Murray's case, tweets contained the word "queers," which he tweeted when he was fourteen and fifteen years old. (What teenager has not said or done something immature, insensitive or stupid?)

Secondly, if any of these had made these statements today, are they not entitled to have *their own* opinion? Do they/we have to *all* agree on *all* matters or just this one?

Another comedian came to Kevin Hart's (who is African American) defense and showed old tweets of three Caucasian female comedians who had tweeted what is considered "homophobic."

In addition, another comedian pointed out the hypocrisy of the Academy Awards that nominated Mel Gibson for an Oscar last year when he has been guilty of saying racial and homophobic statements.

In viewing how some don't receive backlash while others do, people began to wonder if race played a part. It's easy to jump to that conclusion, whether true or not.

I recall a friend of mine, who is African American, telling me that she witnessed an older Caucasian woman fall, and she said she laughed and did not help her. She said she just couldn't because of all the history.

I was surprised to hear her say this. I told her, "When it comes to our actions, it's all based on good and evil. Many people have been tricked into believing in the division of Republicans versus Democrats, White versus Black, rich versus poor, etc."

We have to stop looking at things like that and start judging by what is good and evil as God does. If people stopped and asked themselves "Are my actions good or evil?" before they acted or spoke, there wouldn't be racism and discord.

I told her had the older Caucasian woman fallen in my presence, I would have seen an elder who could have been hurt and needed assistance, and I would have helped her in any way I could.

I hope people wake up and discover racism is ignorance. So is judging a book by its cover. We are humans who have a lot in common, and we would discover that if we took time to talk and understand one another.

Another article dealt with Kobe Bryant who recently won an Oscar but was barred from the Film Academy and won't be granted entry into the Academy of Motion Picture Arts and Sciences. In addition, many thought he should be stripped of his Oscar Nomination for *Dear Basketball* on grounds of his 2003 sexual assault case, a case that was dropped and that he wasn't charged for. And he was removed as a judge of *Hollywood's Animation Is Film Festival* after advocates of the #Metoo movement launched a change.org petition demanding that he be removed due to a "2003 rape *accusation,*" not a charge but an *accusation.*

As a result of the "accusation," he settled a civil suit. This was a highly publicized incident that brought humiliation, undue publicity, and shame to his wife, children, team, franchise, endorsers, etc. In addition, it affected his marriage, life, image, endorsements, etc.

I say this to say that what happened fifteen years ago was atoned for through the civil suit for the "*alleged victim*," through his uphill battle to regain/restore his wife's trust and to save his marriage, to clean his tarnished image, through the loss of endorsements and all other things he went through as a result of his transgressions. (Whether the incident was consensual or not, it was clearly adultery, and he suffered for that, was forgiven by his wife, and atoned for it in many ways).

The difference between Kobe Bryant's situation and others was that he atoned for what he had done. It wasn't hidden, done in the dark, covered up, etc., as the other #Metoo offenders were. For a long time, what they had committed against the vulnerable had gone unreported, hadn't been addressed, or the person had been protected by powerful people in the industry, while victims suffered the end of their careers for blowing the whistle.

So why do people still think it's okay to punish him for what he's atoned for? Must he be punished for the rest of his life? Should we all be punished for the rest of our lives? Does anyone deserve forgiveness? Do prisoners deserve to be punished for their crimes after they have done their time?

I dare those who hide behind their Twitter accounts, those who hurl insults and who sign petitions to forever punish and hold accountable those who have offended, to examine themselves.

It seems people want certain people to issue an apology, extend tolerance, acceptance, sympathy, and inclusion, but there is no atonement, mercy, acceptance, tolerance, or forgiveness for others.

Many are making others feel like they can't have an opinion and will send hateful tweets to bully someone into an apology; example, Kevin Hart, who said he would not issue *another* apology and then did.

This, too, is bullying. When Christians and others are getting thrown in jail, fired, and taken to the Supreme Court or denied a promotion or a job in the NFL, it is bullying to make them conform or pay the price.

In this day and age, nonsense is garnering so much attention and is consuming a lot of our time as we reach a heightened sensitivity level. We need to be mindful of spreading rumors (whether true or false), bearing false witnesses, and assassinating someone's character.

On social media platforms, whenever a story appears, an opinion is expressed, a comment is made, a photo is posted, etc., immediately, court is in session, all judges appear to preside over the case, jurors are selected, and a stiff sentence is handed down, without legal representation.

In most cases, no mercy/leniency is given. Appeals are denied and, generally, a person is convicted versus exonerated as it plays out in public court/domain.

We shouldn't have to constantly apologize for having an opinion in which we are entitled to. We don't have to take everything back. What happened to "Say what you mean and mean what you say?"

Democrats and Republicans agree on some things but not all things. Whites and Blacks agree on some things but not all things. The same thing applies to males and females, children and parents, husbands and wives, students and teachers, etc. Christians disagree with other Christians sometimes. Muslims disagree with other Muslims sometimes. So you have division within many areas, and it's okay, but let us look for common ground and compromise when possible.

There is so much division, backlash, insults, and bullying tactics, etc., used on social media platforms. A lot of people defriend over small things. Twitter wars, old posts resurface to cause humiliation.

If you say something about an artist, the millions of followers of that person will, in concert, attack you as they hide behind their digital devices/vices.

I often wonder how many followers Jesus would have and how many would *defriend* or *befriend* him as the world changes.

It's written, "Follow me as I follow Christ," but you see all these athletes, entertainers, and celebrities with hundreds of thousands, even millions, of followers who are not following Christ, and people are elevating those whose actions, speech, and lyrics do not reflect Christ or anything good at times.

All the social media giants need to be responsible and more vigilant to deter and reduce bullying, overly aggressive, mean-spirited racist behavior by suspending an account for a specific time and, ultimately, altogether to minimize this behavior.

Preventive measures should be taken to ensure their platform is used in a healthy way. We all should be held accountable for the part we play in cultivating this unhealthy environment.

No accountability has led to misuse of the platform, bullying, and increased suicides. (See the RIP section at the end).

> We all should be held accountable for the part we play in cultivating this unhealthy environment. No accountability has led to misuse of the platform, bullying & increased suicides. (See R.I.P. at the end).

We now live in a world where you can do right 99 percent of the time, but as soon as you commit a major mistake, people will quickly forget all that you've done right and will focus on that one mistake versus your body of work. One incident should not define us. Thank God there is only one, true, righteous judge that judges all of us.

On that same note, we should not define God by one thing. I've heard people say when this particular thing occurred, they stopped going to church, turned away from God, or stopped believing in Him.

I've been rebellious at times and then I've asked myself, *How dare you have that attitude with God after all he has done, is doing, and will do for you?* I think of how he has blessed me and shown me favor, then I humble myself, repent, ask for forgiveness, and regroup.

Rebellion against God does us a great disservice and is not conducive to our well-being, walk, or relationship with him.

CHAPTER 9

I read an article where they spoke of a young man who they said had turned a dream "she had since age two into a reality this past June." The article went on to read that the young man recalled a specific conversation "she had with her mother."

"When I was two years old, I went up to my mom and asked her, 'When is the good fairy going to come with her magic wand and change my penis into a vagina?' She said, 'After years of taking hormone blockers and hormone therapy, I've gone through the whole medical process, and this is really the last thing that will validate my identity as a woman.'" This is what the young man said according to the article.

In addition, I read an article where the same boy, now eighteen years old, stressed his fear of approaching puberty, with the expectation of growing facial hair and people learning of his true identity. His parents assured him that they would get the hormones and therapy to prevent this from occurring.

I've never heard of a two-year-old who had penis and vagina in their vocabulary, knew these two determined gender, possessed awareness of what each was, could form a complete sentence and with a complex subject matter, and would remember a conversation from that age. Further, if these words were in his vocabulary at two years of age, what had he been exposed to, who exposed it, and why?

Many of you may have recently heard that an eight-year-old boy, who had just came out to his mother, went to school to share with his classmates, expecting the same support. After being bullied for four days after sharing, he took his life.

In recent years, we have heard of stories of kids younger than this who have come out and made the decision to live as the opposite of what they were born as, and parents are letting them live the life they choose, even going as far as changing the child's name, the way they dress, taking hormones, and having surgery. (At www.sexchangeregret.com, Walt Heyer, seventy, tells his story of being dressed as a girl since the age of three by his grandmother. He continued to follow his grandmother's actions up to having his sex changed and living as a woman. He later reversed as much as he could and went on to author several books to help others. I heard an interview with him on a Christian radio station, along with another story that involves a messy custody battle of a six-year-old boy. The boy's mother insisted her son is transgender and had him wear dresses when he was with her and claimed the dad is cruel for not letting the boy be who he wants to be. The father denied his son is transgender and claimed he doesn't want to wear dresses and desires to dress and be a boy. Currently, the possibility of his father losing custody exists. This is where the law you serve/uphold matters.)

Why are parents allowing their toddlers and young children to make these life-changing decisions at such a tender age? If you allow them to make such a decision at a young age, do you or can you draw a line if they want a tattoo, to smoke weed, or to get their tongue, nipple, or something pierced?

I'm not the judge, and I've never presided over a case, so throughout this writing, I'm continuing to point out the difference between the law of the Lord and the law of the land.

I feel it's important because Kim Davis of Kentucky was thrown in jail for refusing to issue a marriage license for a same-sex couple because it went against her religious beliefs.

Jack Phillips, the owner of a bakery in Colorado, and Charlie Craig and his partner, David Mullins, have been embroiled in a Supreme Court case because the owner refused to create a wedding cake for them. Most businesses reserve the right to refuse service, but this matter was taken to the Supreme Court.

We have many examples of Christians being attacked in other countries, and we have some examples in this country, but the momentum will pick up, so I'm just preparing and placing things on your mind for this coming day.

Back then, they sought reasons to accuse Jesus and his followers, which is why they set up the law to have the three thrown in the fire, and they will continue to seek after his followers in this day.

Are we prepared to stand our ground?

Again, I don't know why this matter and the matter of abortion have gone to the Supreme Court when the Supreme Judge has told us his law governing these matters which reveals the two laws I speak of, the law of the LORD and the law of the land.

I'm not interjecting my opinion, but we were told a STANDARD would be lifted up (referring to a shield, but Jesus is the STANDARD) so we have a Standard in which to compare all matters and don't have to lean on our own understanding or the Supreme Court.

Again, we all are sinners and fall short of the glory and are only saved by grace.

> [A]nd he said unto me, My grace is sufficient for thee. (2 Cor. 12:9)

> [B]ut where sin abounded, grace did much more abound. (Rom. 5:20)

In the beginning, it is understandable how the serpent was able to trick Eve into disobeying God because she was the first lady and didn't have human examples to follow.

We have thousands of years of examples. Before God created mankind, he created all living things and gave them the first commandment, which is to be fruitful and multiply. Upon creating Adam and Eve, they were given the same command. The serpent knew this was a very important commandment because it was the first commandment God gave, and he gave it to all living things in the water, air, ground and man, so he immediately sought to get them to break the commandment.

This brings me to what has been called the Forbidden Fruit and the destruction of Sodom and Gomorrah.

When I was growing up, people said the fruit that had been eaten was an apple, and that's why Adam had the Adam's apple. Eve committed the first sin, so if the sin involved the consumption of an apple, and Eve ate first, wouldn't she have the equivalent of Adam's apple—Eve's apple? It's nonsense.

While I explain, keep in mind that the first commandment to everything that has breath is to be fruitful and multiply, so the serpent sought to trick them into breaking it immediately.

The act was so heinous God said he would curse the serpent to go the rest of his days on his belly and cursed Eve in childbearing, and he put enmity between the serpent and her and between her seed and his seed. (I have another writing in which I go thoroughly into the garden, what this sin was, the enmity between the seeds, and the first will be last and the last shall be first, the evidence in the enmity between the seeds as seen in Cain and Abel, Esau and Jacob, Ishmael and Isaac, Joseph and his brothers, Ham, the father of Canaan, and his two brothers, etc.)

Two men cannot be fruitful and multiply. Two women cannot be fruitful and multiply. Man and beast cannot be fruitful and multiply, nor can anyone bear fruit through sodomy. In addition, in light of new abortion laws, I must say, nor does abortion or forms of birth control replenish the earth.

If we are following God, we must make better decisions prior to committing an act that produces life.

Again, as I pointed out about the rainbow being a sign of God's covenant with mankind, the LGBTQ using it as a symbol contrary to what God said is an abomination.

> These six *things* doth the LORD hate: yea, seven *are* an abomination unto him: A proud look, a lying tongue, and hands that shed innocent blood, An heart that deviseth wicked imaginations, feet that be swift in running to mischief, A false witness *that* speaketh lies, and he that soweth discord among brethren. (Prov. 6:16–19)

Therefore, all is sin in the sight of God, and one is not worse than the other. The only reason the subject of alternative lifestyle is written about more than some of the other subject matters is because there are so many stories in the news as of late and so many laws are being changed, but all subjects mentioned are written in the Bible.

In the world, there are several places throughout where incest, prostitution, bestiality, and same-sex marriage are legal, as well as several drugs that are deemed "small amount for personal use."

While on the subject of marriage, married people know a marriage is work. The reason I point this out is to remind people of the marriage of the Lamb and the church (the body of Christ) so saints know they must work on this marriage/union.

There is a day man dedicated for people to express love, where people go all out. They plan a romantic candlelight dinner and give diamonds and other jewelry, chocolate, roses or other flowers, etc. If man devotes Valentine's Day to express love to a loved one, can't we find ways to reciprocate love to God?

> What shall I render unto the LORD *for* all his benefits toward me? (Ps. 116:12).

No one likes a one-sided relationship, and we should reciprocate God's love.

> For God so loved the world, that he gave his only begotten Son, that whosoever believeth in him should not perish, but have everlasting life. (John 3:16)

How many are married and only communicate with their spouse when times are hard or when they need something? Then why would some choose to only talk to God under those circumstances?

> [A]nd I saw, when for all the causes whereby backsliding Israel committed adultery I had put her away, and given her a bill of divorce; (Jer. 3:8)

[T]urn, O backsliding children, saith the LORD;
for I am married unto you. (Jer. 3:14)

Return, ye backsliding children, *and* I will heal
your backsliding. (Jer. 3:22)

I don't know about you, but I don't want a bill of divorce from God, and I didn't come this far for naught.

Since God is married to the backslider, let us turn from our backsliding and meet him at the altar to renew our vows, making sure we have a relationship and not a religion.

Recently, I listened to "Love Don't Live Here Anymore"; and as many times as I have listened to it, I heard a line that stood out: "When you lived inside of me / there's nothing I could conceive / that you wouldn't do for me." I *thought* I heard "when you lived inside of me / there's nothing I couldn't see / that I wouldn't do for you," and I was thinking if God lives in us, it should be the same way. When he lives inside of us, there should be nothing that we couldn't see that we wouldn't do for him. I had to make sure I quoted lyrics correctly, so I looked them up and realized what I typed above, and then I read the rest of the lyrics and pictured "Love" being God, as he is, and then the lyrics took on another meaning.

When God abides in you and you in Him, there's nothing that you can conceive that he wouldn't do for you, according to his will and his riches. But the lyrics also say, "You abandoned me / found another place to stay / another home," which reminded me of Matthew 22:1–14 where the people abandoned God and where Jesus spoke in a parable, describing what the kingdom of heaven is like. He mentions a certain king who made a marriage for his son and sent his servants to call those who were bidden to the wedding, but they would not come and made excuses as to why they could not attend.

When the king heard it, he was upset and told his servants to go into the highways and as many as they find, bid them to the marriage. He later mentions, "For many are called, but few chosen."

Chapter 10

Because we are flesh and blood as well as spirit, our flesh can cause us to have doubt and experience moments of insecurity. We can waver and get thrown off track, but understand, this is a trick of the enemy.

Trust and believe God is not going to leave something undone. He is not slack concerning his word. He is not going to start something and not finish (he is Alpha and Omega, the beginning and the end, the first and the last, the author and finisher of our faith). I heard a minister say, "Jesus is man on his mother's side and God on his Father's side." As a man, he was tempted (as in tried), falsely accused, lied on, betrayed, he wept, he was moved with compassion, he got angry, frustrated, etc. He felt the emotions we feel.

> Being confident of this very thing, that he which
> hath begun a good work in you will perform *it*
> until the day of Jesus Christ. (Phil. 1:6)

So don't be discouraged. Don't doubt. Know that God's got you and loves you. It's not his will that any should perish, so he gave us a way of escape, but we must choose the Way.

Remember and keep reminding yourself and others that *the devil is defeated.* Defriend Satan right now! The only reason he hangs around is because we entertain him. It is written, "Resist the devil and he will flee." If he didn't flee, it's because we haven't resisted him. Just because opportunity knocks doesn't mean we have to answer, just like when we see "unknown," "private," or "unavailable" on the Caller ID. We know misery loves company, so he will try to trick you into believing a lie, like he did Eve, telling her, "Surely you won't die." Eve didn't realize there was a spiritual death. He knows God's word. We are warned that he is more subtil than any beast of the field, so we have to be alert. Don't let his devices be your vice. He's a liar and the father of lies.

We have to stop acting like we are defeated, like our backs are against the wall, and like we don't have an advocate to defend us. We have an advocate who fights our battles and a mediator in Jesus.

> My little children, these things write I unto you, that ye sin not. And if any man sin, we have an advocate with the Father, Jesus Christ the righteous: And he is the propitiation for our sins: and not for ours only, but also for *the sins of* the whole world. (1 John 2:1–2)

We have one who makes intercessions for us in the Holy Spirit. We have an avenger in God.

> And shall not God avenge his own elect, which cry day and night unto him, though he bear long with them? I tell you that he will avenge them speedily. Nevertheless when the Son of man cometh, shall he find faith on the earth? (Luke 18:7–8)

The battle isn't ours. Don't fear him or his actions; just keep rebuking him and calling on God.

We have our biblical ancestors as examples. Before Florida and other states exercised the "Stand Your Ground" Law, God's people did.

In these days, the people who impose their "Stand Your Ground" right are the ones who live, but when God's people stood their ground, they were thrown in the fire, incarcerated, beaten, etc.

Shadrach, Meshach, and Abednego stood their ground by refusing to bow down and worship an image that Nebuchadnezzar had set up and was thrown in the fire (Dan. 3:16–18). In Daniel 1: 5, 8, they stood their ground and refused to partake of the king's food and beverage.

Daniel was thrown in the lion's den.

John was thrown in jail and later beheaded.

Steven was stoned to death.

> And fear not them which kill the body, but are not able to kill the soul: but rather fear him which is able to destroy both soul and body in hell. (Matt. 10:28)

> In God I will praise his word, in God I have put my trust; I will not fear what flesh can do unto me. (Ps. 56:4)

> [I]f God *be* for us, who *can be* against us? (Rom. 8:31)

Paul was thrown in jail. When Paul was thrown in jail, he didn't sit there sulking, feeling sorry for himself, wondering why God allowed it when he was innocent and doing his work or throw a pity party, expecting friends to RSVP and bring a plus one for visiting hours.

While incarcerated, many prisoners ask the guard, "Did I get any mail today?" Prisoners are usually looking for correspondence with encouraging words from family and friends to keep them strong while on lockdown.

Not Paul. He didn't ask the guard if he had any mail for the day; he handed the guard outgoing mail. He could have been in his cell lifting weights to strengthen his body, but rather he wrote to strengthen another body—the body of Christ, choosing the good part that was needful as Mary had. He didn't concentrate on his situation of confinement physically because he was free spiritually. He wrote to those who were free physically BUT were bound spiritually through sin.

He wrote letters to Timothy, who he referred to as being his son in the faith, to Titus, who he referred to as his son after the common faith, to Philemon, who he referred to as his fellow laborer, to Apphia and Archippus, his fellow soldiers, to the Hebrews and Romans and to the churches—the Corinthians, Galatians, Ephesians, Philippians, Colossians and the Thessalonians—in which some of us have been members of, having been guilty of the things Paul addressed to each of them.

I know there are many people who know Paul's story prior to conversion from Saul and know Paul described himself as chief of sinners, but I know there are many who don't, so I'll briefly explain.

There was a man name Saul who persecuted Christians and condoned the stoning and imprisonment of them as well.

On the way to Damascus, a light shined on him that was so bright it blinded him. The people who accompanied him saw the light but didn't hear the voice that spoke to him. The voice said, "Saul, Saul, why persecutest thou me?" He realized Jesus was speaking to him. He was told where to go and that he would receive his sight.

Saul's name was blotted out and changed to Paul and written in the Book of Life.

I point this out for two reasons: (1) to explain who Paul was prior to being converted to those who may not be familiar with his story and (2) to explain the following to those who have been converted.

Believers know that we have a converted Paul who is no longer Saul, the persecutor of Christians. I say this to point out that if you are a converted Paul, you are not to operate as a persecuting Saul by persecuting Christians. If you are in church talking about another church member in a negative fashion, sowing discord, you are a converted Paul operating as the former man, persecutor Saul, and Jesus is asking you, "Why persecutest thou me?" What Jesus is letting us know is when you attack the body of Christ, you are attacking him. If this is you, repent and make amends.

> Likewise, I say unto you there is joy in the presence of the angels of God over one sinner that repenteth. (Luke 15:10)

Fast-forward to today, Kim Davis stood her ground and was thrown in jail for refusing to issue same-sex marriage license because like the ones above, it was against her faith in God.

You should expect adversity from your adversary.

Know that there is a spiritual war going on, and if you have not been, you will be tried.

> You should expect adversity from your adversary.

Beloved, think it not strange concerning the fiery trial which is to try you, as though some strange thing happened unto you: But rejoice, inasmuch as ye are partakers of Christ's sufferings; that, when his glory shall be revealed, ye may be glad also with exceeding joy. If ye be reproached for the name of Christ, happy *are ye;* for the spirit of glory and of God rested upon you: on their part he is evil spoken of, but on your part he is glorified. But let none of you suffer as a murderer, or *as* a thief, or *as* an evildoer, or as a busybody in other men's matters. Yet if *any man suffer* as a Christian, let him not be ashamed; but let him glorify God on this behalf. For the time *is come* that judgment must begin at the house of God: and if *it* first *begin* at us, what shall the end *be* of them that obey not the gospel of God? And if the righteous scarcely be saved, where shall the ungodly and the sinner appear? (1 Pet. 4:12–18)

Those are just a few differences in the Word and the world and God's law and man's.

CHAPTER 11

What follows is, in part, what I put at the beginning to make sure it was understood:

Please understand, I am writing from a "WE ALL can do better" place and not a judgmental one, for I'm included or have been at one time in some things mentioned. This is to help somebody who wants help or, as I said, who may feel amputated from the body of Christ who wants to be grafted back in or who has been severed from family.

Remember:

> [I] have no pleasure in the death of the wicked;
> but that the wicked turn from his way and live:
> turn ye, turn ye from your evil ways; for why will
> ye die, O house of Israel? (Ezek. 33:11)

> For we have not an high priest which cannot be
> touched with the feeling of our infirmities; but
> was in all points tempted like as *we are, yet* with-
> out sin. (Heb. 4:15)

Jesus got angry and turned over the tables when exchangers of goods were selling things in the house of prayer. (Anger has its place, but you don't hold on to it.) Jesus wept out of frustration and disappointment because they still lacked faith after seeing him perform so many miracles. He was moved with compassion when he saw the people were like sheep without a shepherd. Jesus asked his Father to remove the cup but not for his will but his Father's. He asked friends to sit with him for moral support during this emotional time as he knew he was getting ready to be betrayed and killed (here, we sense he felt anxiety). As a pastor said, "He was man on his mother's side and God on his Father's side." Because he was man also, he experienced emotions such as we do, which is why we are given the scripture about the High Priest so we know he isn't oblivious to what it's like to be us and go through what we go through.

While it is said, To day if ye will hear his voice, harden not your hearts (Heb. 3:15; emphasis mine)

If my people, which are called by my name, shall humble themselves, and pray, and seek my face, and turn from their wicked ways; then will I hear from heaven, and will forgive their sin, and will heal their land. (2 Chron. 7:14; emphasis mine)

Note: What we must do is joined by *and*, meaning we must humble AND pray AND seek AND turn, then he will hear AND forgive AND heal, so don't think you are damned, can't be saved, and that there is no hope. As long as breath is in you, you can do these things, but don't keep delaying because we aren't promised tomorrow or the next moment. Start with repenting. Just acknowledge that you have sinned against him and ask for forgiveness. Then ask that he help you be who he has planned for you to be to bring him glory. Ask him to come into your life and guide you. I heard a song recently, and the singer asked God to follow him. DON'T do this! You want God leading, not following you. What would you look like leading Jesus?

While on the subject, I'd like to discuss the first part, "If my people which are called by my name."

On the week of September 23, 2018, I was in a bookstore with a relative who was having a discussion with the woman who worked there and who was speaking in a very low voice.

After several minutes, he motioned to me as he said, "You need to hear this."

She then asked as she looked at me with disdain, "Are you a Christian?"

I boldly and proudly said, "yes" because I'm not ashamed of the gospel.

In the secular realm, we take pride in and like to throw around titles, either our own, our spouse's or a friend's or a relative's—"I'm the CEO of…" "I'm the *owner* and *founder* of…" "My husband is the *head surgeon* at…" "My son plays for…" but when it comes to our denomination or what we believe, we say, "I'm not into titles."

I thought of how women start out with their maiden name, then take on their husband's last name, how children start off with their father's, stepfather's, or mother's maiden name. Some are even known by where they live, where they are from, for what they are known for, or what their calling is—Galileans, Babylonians, Corinthians, San Franciscans, etc. His name is *Christ*, and if you are a follower of Christ, you are called by his name—*Christian*. If you are disciplined to his word, you are a *disciple*, so don't say you don't go by titles, but know who you are in Christ.

We are sons and daughters of God and heirs with Jesus.

> [B]EHOLD, WHAT manner of love the Father hath bestowed upon us, that we should be called the sons of God: (1 John 3:1)

> For ye have not received the spirit of bondage again to fear; but ye have received the Spirit of adoption, whereby we cry, Abba, Father. (Rom 8:15)

> For whosoever shall do the will of God, the same is my brother, and my sister, and mother. (Mark 3:35)

We hear of children, pit bulls, and puppies waiting to be adopted and looking for a "forever home."

We have an eternal home, a forever home, having put on Christ and receiving the Spirit of adoption from the Father.

> The Spirit itself beareth witness with our spirit, that we are the children of God: And if children, then heirs; heirs of God, and joint-heirs with Christ; if so be that we suffer with *him*, that we may be also glorified together. (Rom. 8:16–17)

> A GOOD name *is* rather to be chosen than great riches, *and* loving favour rather than silver and gold. (Prov. 22:1)

CHAPTER 12

Since I discussed who we are, I'd like to discuss who Jesus is.

Many of us have heard that you do not see the word *Trinity* in the Bible, as well as the word *rapture*, so I'd like to point to scriptures pertaining to these two words, starting with *rapture*.

While discussing with a friend who is a Jehovah's Witness (JW), she sarcastically asked, "What? Are we going to float up in the air in the clouds or something?" In addition, she said JW believe that when you die, that's it and pointed to the scripture, "ashes to ashes, dust to dust." And they don't believe there is a hell. These scriptures will address each.

> For the Lord himself shall descend from heaven with a shout, with the voice of the archangel, and with the trump of God: and the dead in Christ shall rise first: Then we which are alive *and* remain shall be caught up together with them in the clouds to meet the Lord in the air: and so shall we ever be with the Lord. Wherefore comfort one another with these words. (1 Thess. 4:16–18)

So this addresses the rapture as well as life after death. Here are a few others:

> Who died for us, that, whether we wake or sleep, we should live together with him. (1 Thess. 5:10)

> And when he had opened the fifth seal, I saw under the alter the souls of them that were slain

for the word of God, and for the testimony which they held: And they cried with a loud voice, saying, How long, O Lord, holy and true, doest thou not judge and avenge our blood on them that dwell on the earth? (Rev. 6:9–10)

And, behold, there appeared unto them Moses and E-li'as talking with him. Then answered Peter, and said unto Jesus, Lord, it is good for us to be here: if thou wilt, let us make here three tabernacles; one for thee, and one for Moses, and one for Elias. (Matt. 17:3–4)

Here you have two who died: one was carried and one was buried.

And it came to pass, that the beggar died, and was carried by the angels into Abraham's bosom: the rich man also died, and was buried;

And in hell he lift up his eyes, being in torments, and seeth Abraham afar off, and Lazarus in his bosom. (Luke 16:22–23)

Verses 24–31 should be read as well.

Therefore in the resurrection whose wife shall she be of the seven? for they all had her. (Matt 22:28)

In verse 30, Jesus answers:

For in the resurrection they neither marry, nor are given in marriage, but are as the angels of God in heaven.

> And if I go and prepare a place for you, I will come again, and receive you unto myself; that where I am, *there* ye may be also. (John 14:3)

It is true that the body returns to the ground from which it came, but the spirit doesn't return to the ground. The spirit is what is eternal; it doesn't die.

God formed man from the ground and breathed the breath of life into him, and he became a living soul.

If it is the end after our heart stops, and there's no afterlife, *salvation, resurrection,* and *eternal life* would be void and not mentioned, and we wouldn't be raised in incorruption.

Here are a few references of who Jesus is and addresses what people call *Trinity*:

> And God said, Let us make man in our image, after our likeness:... So God created man in his *own* image, in the image of God created he him; male and female created he them. (Gen. 1:26–27)

We see plurals, *us* and *our*, twice, then back to singular. Take note of John 1:1–2, especially verse 1:

> In the beginning was the Word, and the Word was with God, and the Word was God. The same was in the beginning with God

And 1:14 says,

> And the Word was made flesh, and dwelt among us, (and we beheld his glory, the glory as of the only begotten of the Father,) full of grace and truth.

Compare John 1:7–8 to 1:15, 23 and 30, then compare 1:11 to 4:44.

> I am come in my Father's name, and ye receive me not: if another shall come in his own name, him ye will receive. (John 5:43)

> Let this mind be in you, which was also in Christ Jesus: Who, being in the form of God, thought it not robbery to be equal to God: But made himself of no reputation, and took upon him the form of a servant, and was made in the likeness of men: (Phil. 2:5-7)

Continue reading verses 8–11.

> Jesus saith unto him, I am the way, the truth, and the life: no man cometh unto the Father, but by me. If ye had known me, ye should have known my Father also: and from henceforth, ye know him, and have seen him. Philip saith unto him, Lord, shew us the Father, and it sufficeth us. Jesus saith unto him, Have I been so long time with you, and yet hast thou not known me, Philip? he that hath seen me hath seen the Father; and how sayest thou *then*, Shew us the Father? (John 14:6–9)

Read 10 and 11 also.

> Who hath delivered us from the power of darkness, and hath translated *us* into the kingdom of his dear Son: (Col. 1:13)

> Who is the image of the invisible God, the first-born of every creation: (Col. 1:15)

> LET not your heart be troubled: ye believe in
> God, believe also in me. (John 14:1)

(No one else can say if you believe in God, you should also believe in them.)

Also see Titus 2:13–14.

> For there are three that bear record in heaven,
> the Father, the Word, and the Holy Ghost: and
> these three are one. And there are three that bear
> witness in earth, the spirit, and the water, and
> the blood: and these three agree in one. (1 John
> 5:7–8)

Matthew 16:13–17 explains why some people don't understand who Jesus is and don't understand what they read.

> And without controversy great is the mystery of
> godliness: God was manifest in the flesh, justified
> in the Spirit, seen of angels, preached unto the
> Gentiles, believed on in the world, received up
> into glory. (1 Tim. 3:16)

In verse 13, Jesus asked his disciples, "Whom do men say that I the Son of man am?" In verse 14, they gave various answers. In verse 15, Jesus then asked, "But whom say ye that I am?" In verse 16, Simon Peter answered, "Thou art the Christ, the Son of the Living God." In verse 17, Jesus said, "For flesh and blood hath not revealed *it* unto thee, but my Father which is in heaven." So we learn that we, flesh and blood, cannot reveal certain things to others, regardless of how we explain it, so don't get frustrated and argue when people don't understand. Unless the Father in heaven reveals it, they will not understand.

CHAPTER 13

I've discussed who we are in Christ and who Jesus is and would like to discuss what the Bible is.

> All scripture is given by inspiration of God, and *is* profitable for doctrine, for reproof, for correction, for instruction in righteousness: That the man of God may be perfect, thoroughly furnished unto all good works. (2 Tim. 3:16–17)

In the Bible, there is an account of a woman who had an issue with blood, a health problem, but in today's world, there are people who have an issue with blood, a spiritual problem, because they take issue with us having redemption in the shedding of Jesus's blood.

> But if we walk in the light, as he is in the light, we have fellowship one with another, and the blood of Jesus Christ his Son cleanseth us from all sin. (1 John 1:7)

(We had a spiritual dialysis that cleansed us from all sin through the shedding of Jesus's blood).

On October 4, 2018, I heard a radio minister discussing how the names of Daniel, Hananiah, Mishael, and Azariah were changed from godly names to the pagan names Belteshazzar, Shadrach, Meshach, and Abednego, respectively. (The movie *Roots* came to mind where they changed Kunta Kinte's name to Toby.)

In addition to changing their names, upon hearing the music, they wanted them to fall down and worship a golden image that Nebuchadnezzar, the king, had set up (Dan. 3:4–5).

In the military and in prisons, a reveille (wake-up) is played in the morning, and taps is played in the evening. Taps is played at flag ceremonies too. If you are in the military, you are to stop what you are doing and salute as the music plays. If you are a civilian, you have to stop and stand until it stops playing.

For sporting events, the Star-Spangled Banner, our national anthem, is played.

So in the book of Daniel, people were expected to give reverence when they heard the music by falling down and worshipping. In the military and in prisons, when you hear the music, you have to stop (salute, if military) and stand still until the music stops. In the world of sports, you are expected to stand and give reverence to the music. If you don't reverence the music, you face the music.

Years ago, it dawned on me, *the reason the music is so sinister is because of the minister.*

> If you don't reverence the music, you face the music.

In the music industry, they must worship the minister of music by making music and videos full of sex, drugs, alcohol, violence, division, etc.

In addition, secular artists and producers have bled into the gospel music.

If you are a gospel singer, writer, or producer, ask yourself, "Would David have enlisted secular artists, writers, or producers for his psalms?"

So we see a pattern where the minister of music wants people to reverence his music, and like Shadrach, Meshach, Abednego, Collin Kaepernick, Eric Reid, and others, there's a time and necessary reason to stand your ground.

> For I reckon that the sufferings of this present
> time *are* not worthy *to be compared* with the glory
> which shall be revealed in us. (Rom. 8:18)

In Daniel 3:18, Shadrach, Meshach and Abednego answered,

> But if not, be it known unto thee, O king, that we
> will not serve thy gods, nor worship the golden
> image which thou hast set up.

In other words, "even if I'm going to be thrown in the fire, be it known unto thee…" Kim Davis's actions say, "even if I'm going to be thrown in jail, be it known unto thee…" Collin Kaepernick's actions say, "even if it ruins my career, and I can't play in the NFL, be it known unto thee…"

> So that we may boldly say, The Lord *is* my helper,
> and I will not fear what man shall do unto me.
> (Heb. 13:6)

We are under spiritual attack, and if you do not have the whole armor of God on, you will not be able to withstand the fiery darts of the enemy. This is spiritual warfare.

When you don't agree with an idea, and you put up resistance and fail to adhere, they will implement laws in attempts to make you conform, as they did with Shadrach, Meshach, and Abednego.

If you do not stand up for your beliefs during this spiritual attack, you will be subdued and forced to adhere to false doctrine contrary to your belief and become a POSW. (You may have thought I meant POW for prisoner of war, but I meant POSW for **Prisoner of** Spiritual **War**fare.)

Are you willing to stand for your faith?

> He that findeth his life shall lose it: and he that
> loseth his life for my sake shall find it. (Matt.
> 10:39)

I hope, in writing, I have provoked thought, elicited dialogue, and induced labor.

Come unto me, all *ye* that labour and are heavy laden, and I will give you rest. (Matt. 11:28)

(This is a guarantee from the manual)

Let us labour therefore to enter into that rest, lest any man fall after the same example of unbelief. (Heb. 4:11)

[w]ork out your own salvation with fear and trembling. (Phil. 2:12)

The words *labour* and *work* let us know we have work to do. *Labour* implies it's not just work but that the work will be hard, tedious, painful, uncomfortable, etc., like a woman travailing.

I could go on and on about the manual God has given the world (all that inhabit the earth), but my desire is to implore you to look through your own daily ("give us this day, our daily bread," for we aren't promised tomorrow, so get your *daily* bread) so you will be enriched and strengthened as you go through your day/week/walk.

There is life in the word, and if you study enough, it will grow in your heart, mind, and spirit and will manifest in your thoughts, speech, behavior, relationships, etc., and you will reap benefits and so will others who are impacted by your Christlike character.

CHAPTER 14

Years ago, I called a friend a few times and didn't get an answer, so I went to his house to see what was up. Upon arriving, I learned he was okay.

As the years went by, I thought of the many people whom I've heard complain about how they had prayed and prayed and didn't get an answer.

When you pray and pray and don't get an answer, sometimes, you have to go to his house.

CHAPTER 15

Some of us need Jesus "knocking like the police" or to kick in the door, but Jesus stands at the door and knocks; he doesn't just come in and rule your life.

When you answer, open the door and invite Jesus to abide in you, don't treat him like a houseguest, informing him of the "house rules," but relinquish your reign and allow him to rule so he can be glorified in you. He is to rest, rule, and abide in your life.

The kingdom of God is within you, and the body is the temple, so don't let ungodly squatters squat, shack up, and dwell in you.

Chapter 16

In this day and age, if you speak against a certain lifestyle, you are reprimanded, have to issue an apology, are fired, or treated like they treat people who have burned the Bible, Qur'an, or flag or someone who has committed blasphemy against something sacred. So as I was writing, I realized there would be many who will be offended, and that I would come under attack, but when I decided to pick up my cross and follow God, it meant I had made my spiritual bed and would have to lie in it, even if it means being stoned like Stephen, thrown in jail like Paul, or beheaded like John. I also know those offended take offense with God and his word, and not me (the messenger). I don't hear of people attacking FedEx and UPS deliverers because of what they delivered. At any rate, I stand by the message I have delivered, for it is aligned with the Word.

You may have noticed the absence of a Table of Content. The reason is because it started as letters (epistles) to my family and friends and was extended to my neighbors, church members, coworkers and all saints, and whosoever should have an open mind to read, hear, and heed.

Chapter 17

May God bless you richly that your cup runneth over with joy in your heart, peace in your mind, strength in your body, love in your relationships, an attitude of gratitude, graduation in education, a wealth of health, promotion in occupation, lovingkindness, meekness, humility and patience in your character, faith, understanding and discernment in your spirit, and insight in your eyesight.

> And he said, Unto you it is given to know the mysteries of the kingdom of God: but to others in parables; that seeing they might not see, and hearing they might not understand. (Luke 8:10)

As I have ended a couple of my other writings: you'll either succumb or overcome; the choice is yours. (Choose ye this day whom you will serve.)

Read the manual is said that you might be fed. Remember, *study* the WORD and not the world, until those who are scattered have been gathered.

Let us hear the conclusion of the whole matter:

> Fear God, and keep his commandments: for this is the whole *duty* of man. (Eccles. 12:13)

> Now unto him that is able to keep you from falling, and to present *you* faultless before the presence of his glory with exceeding joy, to the only wise God our Saviour, *be* glory and majesty, dominion and power, both now and ever. Amen. (Jude 1:24–25)

Acknowledgments

God the Father, thank you for your love, patience, temperance, mercy, and grace (seen and unseen), favor and blessings (seen and unseen), for protection (seen and unseen) and guidance. Thank you for pouring out your Spirit and using me as an audible voice and vessel. Thank you for the gift of reconciliation and the gift you wrapped in me.

God the Son, thank you for becoming flesh, dwelling among man, giving us the perfect example to follow in order that we might have life and live more abundantly, laying down your life, being wounded for our transgressions, bruised for our iniquities, rising up so whosoever believeth in you would not be condemned but have everlasting life, for going to prepare a place for us and for returning one day nigh to put the adversary under your footstool and gathering your people to our Father.

God the Holy Spirit, thank you for translating the thoughts and desires of my heart to spiritual tongue to reach God when I can't articulate or find the words to express myself.

Thanks to my family, who are blood, and my extended family, who are blood through Christ Jesus, for your prayers and words of encouragement.

Thank you, Nicole, for your encouragement and support as you were the first I shared this writing with. A few of you know I was struggling with a title for it as well as having trouble with the page numbering. It was Nicole who pointed out the most fitting title, which she noticed as she looked through the table of contents of my poetry book as it is the title of a poem I wrote in the '90s. Thanks again.

Once the title was selected, within a day or two, I decided I would pay tribute to my grandmother, Mrs. Ida Dinkins, by using the Bible that belonged to her prior to her homegoing in April 2017.

Thanks to my cousins, Lillian and Betty, Aunt Lillie, and to my sisters in Christ, Valerie and Candace D., for your encouraging words and support, and to all others who read the initial writing before it evolved into the book it is today. It was your encouraging words that gave me strength as I continued to write what God had placed on my heart.

I usually write, type, print, and share with a few relatives, friends, coworkers, etc. (generally about 15–20), but it was at the urging of my cousin Lillian, Aunt Lillie, and my mother, respectively, to protect it that I decided to copyright and eventually publish.

As it began to evolve barely into thirteen pages to a full thirteen pages, I could see that this writing differed from my usual writing and that God intended it to be widely distributed as he continued to pour into my spirit.

Thank you, Pastor McCray, for studying to show thyself approved, rightly dividing the word, being an obedient servant of God and feeding God's flock in two places. May God continue to protect your travels as you preach in both cities, strengthen you to study and deliver two sermons, and provide all that comes with the responsibility it takes to do so. Thank you for your devotion to his flock.

Thanks, Gwen, for providing the instrument that enabled my written word to manifest to print.

REST IN PEACE (GONE WAY TOO SOON)

Gabriel Taye (eight years old) had been the victim of bullying, committed suicide two days after being beaten and left unconscious in a Cincinnati, Ohio, school.

Jamel Myles (nine years old) committed suicide after coming out and being bullied for four days by his classmates in Denver, Colorado.

Madison "Maddie" Whitsett (nine years old) committed suicide after being bullied by classmates who called her "dumb" and "stupid" in Birmingham, Alabama. Coupled with that, Madison had been taking a new medication for ADHD and may have experienced suicidal thoughts, something the maker calls "a side effect."

Your lives mattered and this country should have done and should be doing more about bullying.

The National Suicide Prevention Lifeline and Vets Crisis Line: (1-800-273-8255) 24 hours a day

Substance Abuse and Mental Health Services Administration Helpline: 1-800-662-HELP (4357)

Partnership for Drug-Free Kids 1-855-378-4373 or text 55753

ABOUT THE AUTHOR

Many years ago, God removed the veil from her eyes, and she began to see the world as it truly is. As she often tells people, "I'm able to see more because I look at things from my insight and not my eyesight." What she saw was disturbing, and shortly thereafter, her feelings started to manifest in the form of raps and poems, which later led her to self-publish a poetry book.

Over the years, her writings evolved into essays that she would write, type, print, and share with family and close friends.

As God continued to pour into her spirit, a thirteen-page essay turned into this book.

Therein, she highlights some of the differences between two similar words: the Word and the world—which are completely contrary to another—and the two laws by which man is governed: the law of the Lord and the law of the land.

It is vital to understand the difference so one will realize that a choice exists that one must make.

All that she has written is inspired by the word of God and her spiritual journey.

In writing, she hopes to provoke thought, elicit dialogue and research, and induce labor that causes one to travail and exercise one's gifts, which bring forth good works that are holy and acceptable in God's sight.

She hopes that the reader will be richly blessed and will discover the Truth as they diligently seek it.

CPSIA information can be obtained
at www.ICGtesting.com
Printed in the USA
LVHW111453290721
693918LV00005B/845